COOKING
WITH
KATHERINE WISE

COOKING
WITH
KATHERINE WISE

Resident Chef for KOMO since 1947

KATHERINE WISE

Foreword by KEITH JACKSON

Peanut Butter Publishing
Mercer Island, Washington

Cover Photograph: Rusnak/Leonardi Photography
Production Coordinator: Lee Shepard
Design: Carol Naumann and Greg Harding
Production and Illustration: Jeff Pollard
Production Assistant: Elizabeth Marshall
Typesetting: April Ryan
Copy Editing: Elaine Lotzkar and Heidi Oman

ISBN 0-89716-133-5

Dedication

To my family and all my loyal listeners.

CONTENTS

FOREWORD

The year was 1954. A lean ex-Marine was given his first opportunity in the burgeoning new industry of television. Fresh off the campus of (then) Washington State College, he walked into KOMO in the big city of Seattle with eyes as big as turkey platters. Having to wait two weeks for his beloved young bride to join him, this young man was both scared half to death and thrilled to the heavens to be where he was.

There were many kind people at KOMO to make the beginning easier than one could have hoped; Herb Robinson, Howard Ramaley, Merle Severn, Dave Crockett, Ed Lackner and many others. Most importantly, there was a kind gentle lady from Nebraska who very quietly offered a cup of coffee and conversation about the city, KOMO and living and working in the broadcast industry. It was a pleasure to meet "Katherine Wise" early in my career and I was flattered she had taken the time to talk with a Georgia cracker named Jackson. I liked her immediately because she had the same kind of roots I had. She had come from the country and she had made her way to the top.

Few of us from those days will ever forget how many times the Katherine Wise kitchen provided us with energy during the long days when we were helping build the television industry in Seattle. I also remember how she could scold one fiercely if she found her kitchen messy, but she never cut off the supply of goodies.

During my decade at KOMO it was easy to see the huge impact this lady had on her community. I never saw her back down from a challenge. In fact, she sometimes took a rolling pin attack on agencies controlling consumer products. And she almost always won!

Television eventually took me away from Seattle, but the ten years spent at KOMO are still with me. The pleasure of having the kind gentle lady from Nebraska as a friend is greater than ever.

This book is her gift to all of us. The kind of gift you would expect from Katherine Wise, a simple basic necessity to make one's life happier.

Enjoy, and then you will be like the rest of us who have followed her culinary suggestions—you won't be lean either!

Keith Jackson

Appetizers

Snow Crab Appetizers

1 can snow crab & liquid
1 (8 ounce) package cream
  cheese
1 tablespoon lemon juice
1 teaspoon onion powder

1 teaspoon horseradish sauce
¼ teaspoon salt
Crackers or thinly sliced
  dark bread

Mix the snow crab and liquid with the cream cheese, lemon juice, onion powder, horseradish sauce, and salt. Chill. Place in a serving bowl on a platter with a serving knife. Surround with crackers or thinly sliced dark bread.

Serves 10 to 12.

Artichoke-Mushroom Appetizer

2 (6 ounce) jars artichoke
  hearts
1 (4 ounce) can mushroom
  stems & pieces
1 small onion, finely chopped
1 clove garlic, minced
4 eggs, slightly beaten
¼ cup dry bread crumbs

¼ teaspoon salt
¼ teaspoon Italian seasoning
⅛ teaspoon pepper
⅛ teaspoon hot pepper sauce
2 cups grated or shredded
  sharp cheddar cheese
2 tablespoons dried or
  fresh parsley

Drain the marinade from one jar of artichoke hearts into a frying pan. Drain a second jar. Drain the mushrooms. Chop both the artichokes and mushrooms; set aside. Sauté the finely chopped onion and minced garlic for 5 minutes in the marinade. Add the artichokes and mushrooms. Combine the slightly beaten eggs and the remaining ingredients. Add to the artichokes, mushrooms, onion, and garlic. Lightly press into a 9-inch square baking dish. Bake at 325° for 30 minutes or until set when lightly touched. Let cool for 5 minutes. Cut into tiny squares and serve. Reheat in foil if necessary.

Serves 8-10.

APPETIZERS

KOMO AM1000

Onion & Cheese Goodies

1 cup flour
½ cup butter, softened
½ pound sharp cheddar
   cheese, grated

½ teaspoon salt
½ package onion soup mix

Cream the flour and butter. Blend in the grated cheese, salt, and onion soup mix. Mix well and shape into a roll ½-inch in diameter. Wrap in wax paper and chill. Cut into ⅜-inch slices. Bake at 350° for 8-10 minutes.

Makes about 3 dozen.

Scramble (Nuts & Bolts)

½ cup margarine or butter
1 cup fresh bacon fat or
   salad oil
1 tablespoon salt
1 tablespoon onion salt
1 tablespoon garlic salt
½ teaspoon Tabasco sauce
2 tablespoons Worcestershire
   sauce

1 (16 ounce) package
   Rice Chex
1 (12 ounce) package
   Corn Chex
1 (10 ounce) package thin
   pretzel sticks
½ (18 ounce) package Wheat
   Chex and Raisins
½ (14 ounce) package
   Cheerios
2 cups peanuts

Melt the butter and bacon fat. Add the following seasonings: salt, onion salt, garlic salt, Tabasco sauce, and Worcestershire sauce. In a large roasting pan, combine the Rice Chex, corn chips, thin pretzel sticks, Wheat Chex, Cheerios, and peanuts. Pour the warm seasoning mix over the cereal combination while stirring. Stir to coat as much of the cereal as possible. Bake in an open roasting pan at 200° for about 2 hours, stirring and turning occasionally. The secret is to coat all the cereal with the seasoning. Let dry on brown paper or paper towels. Store in jars or tins. Warm before serving. Refrigerate if stored for any length of time.

Serves 1 football team.

4

Saucy Cocktail Meatballs

2 pounds ground beef
4 tablespoons bread crumbs
2 eggs, slightly beaten
1 teaspoon salt
⅔ cup chopped green pepper
⅔ cup chopped onions
4 tablespoons butter

2 (10¾ ounce) cans tomato
  soup, undiluted
4 tablespoons brown sugar
8 teaspoons Worchestershire
  sauce
2 tablespoons mustard
2 tablespoons vinegar

Mix the ground beef, bread crumbs, eggs, and salt together. Shape into very small meat balls and place in a shallow pan. Broil until brown, turning once. In a saucepan, cook the green pepper and onion in the butter until tender. Then add the tomato soup, brown sugar, Worcestershire sauce, mustard, and vinegar. Pour over the meatballs in the casserole, cover, and bake at 350° for 30 minutes.

Makes about 2 quarts.

Sesame Seed Dip

⅓ cup sesame seeds
1 tablespoon butter
¼ cup grated Parmesan
  cheese
1 cup sour cream
½ cup mayonnaise
1 tablespoon tarragon vinegar

1 tablespoon sugar
1 teaspoon salt
1 clove garlic, mashed
¼ cup minced green pepper
¼ cup minced cucumber
2 tablespoons minced onion
Chips or crackers

Sauté the sesame seeds in butter until lightly browned. Remove from heat and add Parmesan cheese. Blend the sour cream, mayonnaise, and vinegar until smooth. Add the sugar, salt, garlic, green pepper, cucumber, onion, and sesame seed mixture. Serve with chips or crackers.

Makes 2½ cups.

Roasted Pumpkin Seeds

2 cups unwashed
  pumpkin seeds
1 ½ teaspoons salt

½ teaspoon Worchestershire
  sauce
1 ½ tablespoons melted butter

Combine in a shallow pan and bake at 350° for approximately 1 hour. Stir occasionally.

Roasted Sunflower Seeds

Remove the seeds from flowers. Spread in a thin layer on a cookie sheet. Allow to dry overnight. To roast seeds, heat 2 tablespoons oil for each cup of seeds in a heavy skillet. Brown lightly, stirring constantly for about 3 minutes. Pour on to a heavy paper in a thin layer. Allow to cool. Or, heat the oven to 350°. Place the seeds on a cookie sheet and allow seeds to become a delicate brown. Watch carefully and stir if necessary. Cool on the sheet.

Cheese Puffs

½ cup butter or margarine
¼ pound Monterey Jack cheese,
  shredded or very soft
3 ounces cream cheese

1 loaf unsliced bread or
  unbaked rolls
2 egg whites, beaten until stiff

Melt the butter or margarine, Monterey Jack cheese, and cream cheese in a double boiler over very low heat. Trim crusts from a loaf of unsliced bread and cut into 1-inch cubes, or use unbaked rolls. For a large serving, quarter the rolls; for a smaller serving, cut in eighths. Fold the egg whites into the cheese mixture. Dip the cubes in the mixture and place on a waxed paper covered cookie sheet. Place in the freezer. When frozen, put the cubes in a plastic bag and keep in the freezer until ready for use. Bake on a cookie sheet at 400° for 8-10 minutes. If baked without freezing, bake until golden brown.

Cream Cheese Ball

12 ounces cream cheese
½ teaspoon garlic salt
½ teaspoon onion salt

½ green pepper, finely
    chopped (3 tablespoons)
½ cup finely chopped,
    toasted walnuts

Mix the first 4 ingredients. Chill. Roll into a ball. Roll the ball in the toasted walnuts until evenly covered.

Cheddar Cheese Ball

1 pound cheddar cheese,
    grated
6 ounces cream cheese
½ cup sherry
½ cup chopped olives

1 teaspoon Worcestershire
    sauce
Dash each of onion, garlic
    & celery salts
Dried beef, diced

In a bowl, combine cheeses, sherry, olives, Worcestershire sauce, and seasoned salts. Shape into a ball, wrap in foil, and chill. Roll in diced dried beef.

Tangy Cheese Pot

1 pound cheddar cheese,
    grated
1 teaspoon curry powder
1 teaspoon chopped chives
½ teaspoon Dijon mustard

Dash cayenne pepper
½ teaspoon onion salt
⅓ cup dry sherry wine
1 tablespoon vegetable oil

On medium speed, blend until smooth half the cheddar cheese with the curry powder, chives, Dijon mustard, pepper, onion salt, dry sherry wine, and vegetable oil. Add the remaining cheese and blend until smooth. If too thick, add as much of ¼ cup of sherry as needed to give a desired consistency. If you use a mixer, place all the ingredients in a mixing bowl and beat at medium speed until well blended. If the mixture is lumpy, use a large wooden spoon to smooth. Place in an airtight storage container; refrigerate up to one month.

Makes about 3 cups.

Smorgasbord Pie

2¼ cups buttered cracker
   crumbs, finely rolled
2 egg whites, slightly beaten
2 tablespoons butter or
   margarine, melted & cooled
¾ teaspoon unflavored gelatin
2 tablespoons cold water
¾ cup mayonnaise
¾ cup chopped celery

1 (7 ounce) can tuna,
   drained & flaked
1 (2 ounce) jar pimentos,
   sliced & drained
5 hard-boiled eggs, chopped
1 tablespoon minced
   anchovies
½ cup cottage cheese
¼ cup chopped stuffed olives
2 tablespoons chopped
   ripe olives

Blend the first 3 ingredients. Press firmly against the bottom and sides of a 9-inch pie plate. (The easy way is to use an 8-inch pie plate.) Bake at 375°) for 8-10 minutes. Cool. Soften the gelatin in cold water; dissolve over hot water. Add to the mayonnaise and mix well. Combine ½ cup of the mayonnaise mixture with ½ cup chopped celery, tuna, and sliced pimentos. Spoon in a circle next to the edge of the crust. Combine the remaining mayonnaise and celery, hard-boiled eggs, and anchovies. Spoon in a circle next to the tuna salad. Fill the center with cottage cheese. Ring the stuffed olives between the tuna and egg salad and the ripe olives between the egg salad and cottage cheese. Refrigerate for about ½ hour before serving.

Makes approximately 10 (2¾-inch) wedges.

Chinese Cherry Sauced Chicken Wings

3 pounds chicken wings
1 (16 ounce) can or jar dark
   sweet cherries
¼ cup brown sugar
2 teaspoons grated fresh
   ginger root or ½ teaspoon
   powdered ginger

1 small clove garlic, minced
½ cup soy sauce
¼ cup port wine
2 tablespoons lemon juice
2 tablespoons cornstarch

Remove and discard the small tips of the chicken wings. Cut between

8

the main and second wing joints to make 2 pieces from each wing. Place in a glass bowl. Place the cherries with syrup in a blender and blend until smooth. Add the brown sugar, ginger, garlic, soy sauce, port wine, and lemon juice; blend. Pour over the chicken wings and marinate 2 to 3 hours, turning occasionally. Drain, reserving the marinade. Place the chicken wings in a single layer in a baking pan. Bake at 450° for 10 minutes. Turn and bake 10 minutes more. Reduce the temperature to 350°. Continue to bake 20 minutes longer or until tender, brushing 2 to 3 times with reserved cherry marinade. Remaining marinade may be thickened with cornstarch to serve as a dipping sauce.

Makes about 3 dozen portions.

Sweet and Sour Meatballs
Marcia Ransom's *Skinny Gourmet*

2 pounds lean ground beef
1 tablespoon fresh parsley,
   chopped
¼ teaspoon paprika
¼ teaspoon summer savory
2 cups tomato sauce
   (no sugar added)

2 cups unsweetened
   pineapple juice
Juice of 1 lemon, seeded
   & strained
1 tablespoon soy sauce
Salt & freshly ground
   black pepper
Scallions, minced

Combine the beef, parsley, paprika, and summer savory. Blend well. Form into small meatballs about 1½ inches in diameter. In a heavy saucepan, combine the tomato sauce, pineapple juice, lemon juice, and soy sauce. Bring to a boil and carefully drop in the meatballs. Turn each one to coat with the sauce. Cook, covered, at a strong simmer for 20-25 minutes, until the meatballs are done. Stir gently a few times to prevent sticking. Turn each meatball once halfway through cooking. To serve, remove the meatballs from the sauce with a slotted spoon, season with salt and freshly ground black pepper to taste, and sprinkle minced scallions overall.

Serves 6.

Crab Ball Hors d'Oeuvre

1 (6 ounce) package frozen
   Alaska snow crabmeat
1 (8 ounce) package cream
   cheese, softened

2 teaspoons chopped chives
¼ teaspoon garlic powder
¼ teaspoon salt
½ cup chopped pecans

Thaw and the drain crabmeat. Blend the cream cheese, chives, garlic powder, and salt. Fold in the crabmeat. Shape into a log or ball. Roll in pecans. Serve with crackers or fresh vegetables.

Peanut Butter Dip

½ cup creamy peanut butter
½ cup dairy sour cream
¼ cup frozen orange juice
   concentrate, thawed
3 tablespoons finely chopped
   candied ginger

Honeydew and cantaloupe
   melon, cut into
   bite-size cubes
Grapefruit, cut into wedges
Apples, cut into wedges

Combine the peanut butter, sour cream, and orange juice. Stir in the ginger, mixing well. Before serving, stir the peanut butter mixture. Use as a dip for melon cubes, grapefruit, and apple wedges.

Crunchy Party Snacks

½ cup margarine or butter
2 tablespoons Worcestershire
   sauce

4 cups herb-seasoned
   croutons
1 cup cocktail peanuts
1 cup thin stick pretzels

Melt the margarine or butter in a large saucepan over medium heat. Remove from the heat. Stir in the Worcestershire sauce. Add the croutons, peanuts, and pretzels. Toss gently until well combined. Spread the crouton mixture in a large baking pan. Bake at 300° for about 15 minutes or until crisp, stirring occasionally. Serve hot or cooled. To store, place in a tightly covered container.

Makes about 5½ cups.

Sausage and Cheese Balls

3½ cups biscuit mix
1 pound mild sausage

8 ounces cheddar cheese,
  grated
⅓ cup butter, melted & cooled

Combine the biscuit mix, sausage, and cheese. Mix until well blended. Add the melted, cooled butter. Work together well, allowing to come to room temperature. Shape into small balls. Place on an ungreased cookie sheet. Bake at 350° for 20 minutes.

Note: These freeze well.

Makes about 5 dozen appetizers.

Cheesy Cream Dip

¾ cup shredded cheddar
  cheese
2 tablespoons chopped
  pimento-stuffed olives

¼ teaspoon salt
⅛ teaspoon rubbed sage
1 cup dairy sour cream

In a bowl, gently blend the cheese, olives, salt, and sage into the sour cream. Cover and chill.

Salmon Avocado Spread

1 (7¾ ounce) can salmon
1 avocado, refrigerated
  for 4 hours
1 tablespoon lemon juice
1 tablespoon olive or salad oil

1 clove garlic, finely chopped
1½ teaspoons grated onion
½ teaspoon salt
4 drops Tabasco sauce
Crackers

Drain and flake the salmon. Peel the avocado and chop coarsely. Combine all ingredients and toss lightly. Serve with crackers.

Makes 1 pint.

Smashing Wheat Pretzels

2 cups enriched flour
2 cups whole wheat flour
1 package dry yeast
1 teaspoon salt

1 ⅓ cups warm water
3 tablespoons oil
1 tablespoon honey
Coarse salt

Stir together the enriched and whole wheat flours. (Spoon the flour into a dry measuring cup and level; do not scoop.) Combine 1½ cups flour, yeast, and salt. Add warm water (120° to 130°), oil, and honey to the flour-yeast mixture. Beat until smooth (about 2 minutes). Add enough more flour to make a moderately stiff dough. Knead 3-5 minutes until smooth. Cut into 12 pieces and roll each into a rope 15 inches long. Roll in coarse salt and shape into a pretzel, then place on a greased baking sheet. Bake at 425° for 20 minutes or until lightly browned.

Makes 12 pretzels.

Crab Puffs

1 cup water
½ cup butter or margarine
1 cup flour
4 eggs

Crab Stuffing:
2 cans crabmeat
½ fresh lemon

2 hard-boiled eggs, chopped
1 (8 ounce) package
   cream cheese
Grated onion juice to taste
Dash Worcestershire sauce
Dab mayonnaise
Salt & pepper to taste

In a saucepan, heat the water and butter or margarine to boiling. Add the flour and reduce heat to low, stirring constantly until the mixture forms a ball. Remove from the heat and add the eggs all at once. Beat well until smooth and glossy. Place small teaspoonfuls on an ungreased cookie sheet. Bake at 400° for approximately 20 minutes or until golden brown. Cool and slice tops open to fill with **Crab Stuffing** and replace the tops.
Crab Stuffing: Mix all ingredients together thoroughly.

Makes 6 dozen puffs.

12

Party Spread for Pretzels

1 ½ pounds aged cheddar
  cheese, grated
¼ pound Roquefort cheese,
  crumbled
1 teaspoon dry mustard
2 tablespoons soft butter

1 teaspoon Worcestershire
  sauce
⅛ teaspoon Tabasco sauce
2 teaspoons grated onion or
  finely chopped chives
1 (12 ounce) bottle beer
Parsley
Paprika

Place all the ingredients except for the beer, parsley, and paprika in a large mixing bowl. Let stand for 20 minutes to soften the cheese. With a mixer on low speed, pour in the beer gradually, mixing until all the beer is incorporated and the mixture is smooth and fluffy. Serve in a large bowl sprinkled with minced fresh parsley and paprika. Accompany with pretzel twists or sticks. Excellent with soft pretzels. Store in a tightly covered container in the refrigerator or freezer until needed for a party.

Makes about 5 cups.

Potted Cheese

1 pound aged cheddar
  cheese, grated
½ teaspoon curry powder
¼ cup chopped chives
1 tablespoon Pommery
  mustard

1 ounce cognac
2 tablespoons butter, softened
Rolls, French bread,
  or crackers

Toss the cheese with the curry powder and chives. Blend gradually with the mustard, cognac, and butter. Stir until smooth and spreadable, adding more butter, mustard, or a little cream, if necessary. Pack into crocks or ramekins. Seal tightly with plastic wrap or foil. Store in the refrigerator. Bring to room temperature before serving with whole-grain rolls, French bread, or plain crackers.

Meatball Hors d'Oeuvres

4 cups soft bread crumbs
1 cup milk
⅓ cup Sauterne wine
2 tablespoons soy sauce
1 tablespoon garlic salt
½ teaspoon onion powder

¼ teaspoon ginger
1½ pounds ground beef
½ pound pork sausage
2 (5 ounce) cans water
    chestnuts, drained &
    finely chopped

Combine the bread crumbs, milk, Sauterne, soy sauce, garlic salt, onion powder, and ginger. Add the ground beef, pork sausage, and water chestnuts, mixing well. Form into 1-inch balls. Place on a shallow baking pan and bake at 350° for 30-35 minutes.

Makes 10 dozen.

Cheese English Muffin Puffs

¼ pound butter or margarine
¼ pound Monterey Jack
    cheese, shredded
3 ounces cream cheese

2 egg whites, beaten stiff
6 English muffins or center
    slices of 1 large loaf bread

Melt the butter or margarine, Monterey Jack cheese, and cream cheese in a double boiler over very low heat. Remove from the heat and water. Fold in the egg whites. Cut English muffins into 6 equal pie-shaped pieces. Dip the muffin pieces in the mixture, using a fork for dipping, coating all sides. Place on a waxed paper covered cookie sheet and then freeze. When frozen, put wedges in a plastic bag and keep in the freezer until ready for use. (You may want to use sandwich sliced bread, cut in half. Crusts are optional.) Flow the cheese mixture on the bread, with a spoon, on one side only, then freeze, stack, and wrap. When ready to use, bake on a cookie sheet at 400° for 10-12 minutes or until golden brown. These are excellent with salads or soups and can be used for party finger food.

Freezer Cheese Balls

8 ounces sharp cheddar
  cheese, grated
1 clove garlic, minced
1 (8 ounce) package cream
  cheese, softened

4 ounces bleu cheese,
  crumbled
¼ cup butter or margarine,
  softened
¾ cup coarsely chopped
  walnuts or pecans
Crackers or melba toast

Combine the cheddar cheese, minced garlic, softened cream cheese, crumbled bleu cheese, and softened butter. Mix until well blended. Cover and chill until firm enough to shape. Divide the mixture in half and shape each half into a smooth ball. Wrap air-tight in clear plastic wrap, then place in a plastic bag, and refrigerate or freeze. To serve, let the frozen cheese balls stand at room temperature, unwrapped, 3-4 hours. Roll each ball in nuts, pressing in lightly. Serve with assorted crackers or wafers.

Makes 2 cheese balls about 3 inches in diameter.

Hot Hors d'Oeuvres Spareribs

1 cup white wine vinegar
1 clove garlic, crushed
1 tablespoon olive oil
2½ tablespoons Worcester-
  shire sauce
Dash hot pepper sauce
1 tablespoon sugar
⅓ cup catsup

1 teaspoon dry mustard
1 teaspoon salt
½ teaspoon pepper
½ teaspoon paprika
1 tablespoon soy sauce
2 jars strained baby food fruit
12 pounds spareribs

Combine all ingredients except the spareribs and simmer for 15 minutes. Pour this marinade over the spareribs, cut into individual pieces. Marinate overnight. Pour off the juice and use to baste while baking at 400° for ½ hour. At this point, they may be refrigerated or frozen. When ready to serve, bring to room temperature and place under the broiler until brown and crisp.

Makes about 72 pieces of ribs, depending on the way they are cut.

Coffee Hour Dips

6 slices bacon
2 ripe medium avocados
1 cup dairy sour cream
1 ½ teaspoons onion salt

2 tablespoons horseradish
2 teaspoons lemon juice
1 teaspoon Worcestershire
    sauce

Cook the bacon until crisp and break into small bits. Mash the avocados to a smooth pulp. Add the sour cream, onion salt, horseradish, lemon juice, Worcestershire sauce, and bacon. Combine well and chill. Serve with corn chips, crackers, or as a dunk for celery and carrot sticks.

---

6 ounces cream cheese
1 can deviled ham
1 hard-boiled egg, grated

¼ cup mayonnaise
Salt
Prepared mustard

Soften the cream cheese; blend in the deviled ham, egg, mayonnaise, salt, and mustard to taste.

---

6 ounces cream cheese
¼ cup light cream
¼ cup mayonnaise

1 teaspoon grated onion
1 small can shrimp,
    drained & minced
Salt, pepper, & lemon juice

Soften the cream cheese; add the light cream, mayonnaise, grated onion, shrimp, salt, pepper, and lemon juice to taste. Combine and chill.

Sweet & Sour Cocktail Weiners

1 (6 ounce) jar prepared
  mustard

1 (10 ounce) jar currant jelly
1 pound frankfurters

Mix the prepared mustard with jelly in a chafing dish or double boiler. Slice the frankfurters into bite-sized pieces. Add to the sauce and heat.

Serves 8 to 10.

Deviled Toast Sticks

1 loaf Italian bread
1 cube butter
1 clove garlic, minced
1 teaspoon Worcestershire
  sauce

1 teaspoon prepared mustard
1 tablespoon beefsteak sauce
1 tablespoon poppy seeds
½ teaspoon mixed herbs

Slice the bread into 1-inch thick pieces. Trim the crusts and cut slices into strips 1-inch wide. Melt the butter and add the garlic. Blend in the Worcestershire, mustard, beefsteak sauce, poppy seeds, and mixed herbs. Simmer a few minutes. Dip the breadsticks lightly in the mix. Place on a cookie sheet and bake at 225° until crisp. These sticks can be recrisped just before serving.

Serves 8 to 10.

Sunday Night Cheese Puffs

6 eggs
3 cups milk
2 tablespoons minced parsley
¾ teaspoon dry mustard

½ teaspoon salt
10 slices bread, cubed
2 cups shredded cheddar
  cheese

Beat the eggs, milk, minced parsley, dry mustard, and salt. Stir in the bread cubes and cheddar cheese. Pour into a buttered oblong baking dish. Set the dish into another pan of water. Bake, uncovered, at 325° for 1 hour or until the center is set. Cut into squares and serve.

Serves 6.

Cheese Snacks

1 cup shredded cheddar
   cheese
¼ cup butter, softened
¼ cup toasted sesame seeds
1 egg

1 tablespoon Worcestershire
   sauce
¼ teaspoon hot pepper sauce
1 cup enriched flour

Beat together the cheese, butter, sesame seeds, egg, Worcestershire sauce, and hot pepper sauce until well blended. Stir in the flour. Mix well. Wrap in wax paper and press together. Roll out to a 16-inch log. Chill for easier slicing, about 1 hour. Slice ⅛-inch thick and place on ungreased baking sheets. Bake at 350° for 12 to 15 minutes. Remove from pans immediately. Serve hot or cool.

Makes about 6 dozen.

Parkerhouse Turkey Puffs

1 cup cooked turkey, cubed
¼ cup mayonnaise
¼ cup finely chopped celery
2 tablespoons chopped nuts
1-3 teaspoons soy sauce
½-1 teaspoon curry powder

1 can Parkerhouse Dinner
   Rolls (Refrigerated Quick)

Topping:
1 egg white
⅛ teaspoon cream of tartar
¼ cup mayonnaise

Combine the first 6 ingredients to make the filling. Separate dough into 12 rolls. Place 1 tablespoon of filling in the pocket of each roll and press edges to seal. Place on an ungreased cookie sheet. Prepare **Topping** and place 1 tablespoon on each roll. Bake at 400° for 12 minutes or until the rolls are brown on the edges. Serve warm.

Topping: Whip the egg white with cream of tartar to soft peak stage, then fold in mayonnaise.

If desired, omit the soy sauce and curry powder and substitute 2 tablespoons pickle relish. Cubed ham or cubed chicken may be substituted for turkey.

Cheese Sticks

2 teaspoons salt
4 cups all-purpose flour
¾ cup plus 2 tablespoons
  butter
½ cup lard
1 cup cold water,
  approximately

1 egg
1 tablespoon dry sherry
12 ounces sharp cheddar
  cheese, grated
Cayenne pepper (optional)
Sesame seeds or poppy seeds

Combine the salt and all-purpose flour. Cut in with a pastry blender ½ cup butter and the lard. Add the cold water a few tablespoons at a time, as you do when making pie pastry. Divide in half and chill. Melt 4 tablespoons butter. Beat the egg with dry sherry. Roll out half of the dough to the thickness of pie pastry, trying to shape in a rectangular form. Sprinkle with ½ the grated cheese, covering all the pastry. Dot with 2 tablespoons melted butter. Press cheese onto pastry using your hand. Sprinkle very lightly with cayenne pepper if desired. Fold in thirds. Roll out thin and refold in thirds twice more. Chill, if necessary, and reroll. Cut in 1-inch by 3-inch long strips with a pastry wheel. Brush with the egg beaten with sherry, and sprinkle with either sesame or poppy seeds. Place on cookie sheets. Bake at 400° for 10-12 minutes or until golden and puffy. Do the same with the other half of the pastry. These can be frozen, if packed so they do not break.

Makes 6 to 7 dozen.

Mock Pâté

1 (8 ounce) package cream
  cheese, softened
1 (8 ounce) package liver
  sausage

1 tablespoon chopped onion
1 teaspoon lemon juice
1 teaspoon Worcestershire
  sauce
Dash salt and pepper

Combine the cream cheese and liver sausage, mixing until well blended. Add remaining ingredients. Mix well.

Makes 2 cups.

Party Tuna Pâté

½ cup water
1 tablespoon lemon juice
1 envelope unflavored gelatin
1 (16 ounce) carton
   sour cream
½ cup mayonnaise
¼ teaspoon salt
⅛ teaspoon pepper
⅛ teaspoon hot pepper sauce
2 (7 ounce) cans fancy white
   tuna, drained
½ onion, chopped
½ green pepper, chopped

1 (4 ounce) can red pimento,
   drained
Parsley (optional)

Sour Cream Party Dip:
1 (16 ounce) carton
   sour cream
2 tablespoons snipped parsley
2 tablepoons lemon juice
1 clove garlic, minced
1 teaspoon lemon rind
½ teaspoon onion powder
Dash salt & pepper

In a small saucepan, mix the water and lemon juice. Sprinkle the gelatin over the water; soften 1 minute. Heat to boiling, stirring constantly until gelatin is dissolved. Remove from heat. Reserve. Mix the sour cream, mayonnaise, salt, pepper, and hot pepper sauce. Place the tuna, onion, green pepper, and pimento in a blender container or a food processor with a steel blade. Cover and process until the vegetables are finely minced. Drain excess moisture. Stir into sour cream mixture. Stir in the gelatin. Pour into a 5 cup mold and cover. Refrigerate until firm, at least 3 hours, but no longer than 48 hours. To serve, unmold on a serving plate. Arrange assorted crackers around the mold. Fill the center of the mold with **Sour Cream Party Dip**. Garnish with parsley.

Sour Cream Party Dip: In a small bowl, mix all the ingredients and cover. Refrigerate at least 4 hours or until serving time. Stir before serving.

Makes 5 cups of Pâté and 2 cups Party Dip.

Crock Pot Cheese

1 teaspoon garlic salt
1 teaspoon dry mustard
1 teaspoon Worcestershire
  sauce
2 teaspoons minced onion

Dash Tabasco sauce
1 tablespoon butter
8 ounces beer
1 pound sharp cheddar
  cheese, grated

Have all ingredients at room temperature. Combine the garlic salt, dry mustard, Worcestershire sauce, onion, Tabasco, butter, and beer. Add the grated cheese and beat until smooth and fluffy. Store in a covered container in the refrigerator. Serve at room temperature with crackers or dark bread.

Nutty Appetizer Meat Balls

½ pound lean ground beef
⅓ cup old-fashioned
  peanut butter
1 egg, slightly beaten
2 tablespoons finely
  chopped peanuts
2 tablespoons fine dry
  bread crumbs

1 tablespoon Worcestershire
  sauce
2 teaspoons instant
  minced onion
¼ teaspoon salt
⅛ teaspoon pepper
Chopped parsley for garnish

Combine all ingredients in a bowl. Mix well. Shape the mixture into 1-inch balls. Place in a single layer in a large, shallow pan. Bake at 500° for 5-7 minutes. Place in a chafing or serving dish. Garnish with chopped parsley if desired. Serve hot.

Makes 3 dozen.

Butter Baked Wings and Drumsticks

12 chicken drumsticks
  (3 pounds)
12 chicken wings (2 pounds)
2 teaspoons salt

¼ teaspoon pepper
2 cups soda cracker crumbs
1 teaspoon poultry seasoning
1 cup melted butter

Sprinkle the chicken with salt and pepper. Combine the crumbs and poultry seasoning. Dip the chicken in melted butter, then roll in crumbs to coat well. Place on 2 foil-lined 15½x10½-inch shallow baking pans. Drizzle the remaining butter over the chicken. Bake at 375° for 45-60 minutes or until tender.

Serves 8-12.

Crunchy Peanut Butter Filling for Celery

2 (3 ounce) packages cream
  cheese
⅔ cup crunchy peanut butter
¼ cup milk

¼-½ teaspoon curry powder
⅓ cup sweet-pickle relish
¼ cup chopped pimento-
  stuffed olives

Combine the cream cheese, peanut butter, and milk. Mix until creamy. Add the remaining ingredients and mix well. Store, covered, in the refrigerator. Keeps well for 2 weeks.

Makes about 2 cups.

Seasoned Liver Spread

½ pound liver sausage
3 tablespoons minced
  cucumber chips
¼ cup mayonnaise
2 teaspoons dry mustard

¾ teaspoon Worcestershire
  sauce
⅛-¼ teaspoon Tabasco sauce
Salt to taste

Blend all ingredients well. Serve with crackers or assorted breads.

Makes 1 cup.

Vegetable Spinach Dip

2 cups real mayonnaise
1 (10 ounce) package frozen,
   chopped spinach, cooked
   & drained
½ cup chopped green onion

½ cup chopped parsley
¼ cup pickle relish, drained
1 teaspoon salt
½ teaspoon pepper

Combine all ingredients; mix well. Chill several hours or overnight. Serve with assorted vegetable dippers such as sliced cucumbers, celery sticks, radishes, broccoli, or any fresh spring vegetable.

Salmon Torta Appetizer

1 (7¾ ounce) can pink
   salmon
4 eggs
1½ cups unpared,
   shredded zucchini

¾ cup biscuit mix
½ cup dairy sour cream
½ cup diced onion
1 teaspoon tarragon
½ teaspoon salt

Drain the salmon and combine with the eggs, zucchini, biscuit mix, sour cream, onion, tarragon, and salt. Mix well. Pour into a 1½ quart shallow, buttered, glass casserole dish. Bake at 350° for 30-35 minutes until firm and golden. Cut into bite-size pieces. Serve at room temperature.

Makes 4 to 6 servings.

Avocado Cheese Dip

2 medium avocados, mashed
2 tablespoons lemon juice
½ teaspoon salt
2 tablespoons finely chopped
  onion

2 (3 ounce) packages cream
  cheese, softened
2 tablespoons milk

Combine the avocados, lemon juice, salt, and onion. Combine the cream cheese and milk. Blend the cream cheese mixture into the avocado mixture. Serve as a dip with large size corn chips.

Serves 8 to 10.

Peanut-Ham Dip

½ cup mayonnaise
1 (8 ounce) package
  cream cheese
½ cup finely chopped peanuts
1 (4¾ ounce) can deviled ham

2 tablespoons chopped
  pimento
¼ cup finely chopped
  cucumber chips
¼ teaspoon Worcestershire
  sauce
Dash pepper & paprika

Gradually add the mayonnaise to the cream cheese; blend until smooth. Add the peanuts, deviled ham, pimento, cucumber chips, Worcestershire sauce, pepper, and paprika. Mix well. Serve with potato chips or crackers.

Makes about 3 cups.

Northwest Canapes

3 cups flaked Northwest
  seafood (salmon, crab,
  shrimp, halibut, or cod)
⅔ cup mayonnaise
⅔ cup diced celery
½ cup pickle relish
⅓ cup thinly sliced
  green onions

¼ cup lemon juice
1 tablespoon prepared
  mustard
2 teaspoons Worcestershire
  sauce
¾ teaspoon salt
¼ teaspoon garlic powder

Combine all ingredients, mixing thoroughly. Use as a spread for an assortment of shapes and varieties of bread.

Makes about 4½ cups, enough for approximately 6 dozen small canapes.

25

Beverages

Pink Punch

1 quart cranberry juice
cocktail
1 (46 ounce) can unsweetened
pineapple juice

1 (12 ounce) can frozen
lemonade concentrate
2 quarts ginger ale

Blend all the ingredients except the ginger ale. Chill. Just before serving, stir in the ginger ale. A fifth of vodka or gin may be added if desired.

Makes approximately 4 quarts.

À la Champagne Punch

2 lemons
2 bottles Rhine wine, chilled

2 bottles Chenin Blanc, chilled
¾ quart sparkling water,
chilled

Peel the lemons in wide, unbroken spiral strips, leaving the end of each spiral attached to the lemon. Put the lemons in a large glass punch bowl, and hang the free ends of the peel over the container's rim. Pour in the chilled Rhine wine and chilled Chenin Blanc. Just before serving, add ice cubes and the sparkling water.

Serves 16.

Hot Buttered Rum

2 tablespoons brown sugar
1 teaspoon allspice
1 teaspoon whole cloves
Dash ground nutmeg
3 inches of stick cinnamon

¼ teaspoon salt
2 quarts apple or
    pineapple juice
1 cup rum
½ cup butter

In a large saucepan, combine the brown sugar, spices, salt, and apple or pineapple juice. Slowly bring the mixture to boiling. Reduce heat, cover, and simmer for 20 minutes. Stir in the rum and return just to boiling. Remove from heat and pour through a strainer to remove the whole spices. Place a pat of butter in each of eight mugs. Pour in the hot rum mixture.

Variations: Use wine instead of apple juice and rum; or omit the rum and have an excellent spiced fruit juice.

Serves 8.

Bicentennial Recipe - Fish House Punch

1 cup sugar
3⅓ cups cold water
3⅓ cups lemon juice
1 fifth cognac or brandy
1½ fifths Puerto Rican
    rum (golden)

½ fifth Jamaican rum (dark)
½ pint peach-flavored brandy
    or peach cordial
1 large bottle club soda,
    chilled

Stir the sugar with the water to dissolve. Add the remaining ingredients except club soda. Place in the refrigerator to chill and mellow for several hours or overnight. When ready to serve, pour over a block of ice in a large punch bowl. At the last moment, add the club soda and stir once. Serve in punch cups.

This is a potent brew. Do not confuse it with your typical wedding-reception punch.

Serves 40 to 50.

30

Cocoa Mix

1 cup cocoa
2 cups sugar
5½ cups powdered milk, dry

1 cup powdered non-dairy
   creamer
1½ teaspoons salt

Mix all ingredients together. Store in a jar with a tight lid. To use, put some mix, about 2 rounded teaspoons, in a cup and fill with hot water.

For a holiday treat, add 1-1½ ounce peppermint Schnapps, or simply use a touch of peppermint extract.

Makes approximately 38 cups.

Mexican Chocolate Coffee

½ cup instant coffee
½ cup granulated sugar
1 cup non-dairy creamer
1 cup instant cocoa mix
½ teaspoon each of nutmeg,
   cloves, cinnamon, and
   cardamom

Whipped cream

Mexican Cinnamon Sugar:
1 cup fine sugar
1 tablespoon cinnamon
1 tablespoon cocoa or
   cocoa mix

Mix together all the ingredients in the first column. About 3-4 spoonfuls per mug or cup of hot water will make a nice after-dinner coffee. Top with whipped cream and sprinkle with **Mexican Cinnamon Sugar**.

Mexican Cinnamon Sugar: Mix all the ingredients well. Store in an air-tight container. Can also be used over warm puddings and custards.

Tailgate Punch

1 (4/5) bottle brandy
  (or sweet white wine)
1 (4/5) bottle gin or vodka
1 (26 ounce) bottle champagne,
  sparkling wine, or club soda
3 (6 ounce) cans frozen lemon-
  nade, limeade or grapefruit
  juice concentrate, thawed

½ cup lemon juice
Mint leaves for garnish,
  if available
Maraschino cherries for garnish
3 trays ice cubes
3 (28 ounce) bottles club soda
  or ginger ale, chilled

In a large bowl, mix together the first 3 ingredients. Add the remaining ingredients. (The substitutes also work very nicely). Add ice and soda just before serving. More juice, ice, and soda can be added to taste.

This recipe comes from the 1962 Seattle World's Fair.

Serves 20.

Husky Tea

3 cups sugar
2 cups instant natural orange
  flavored breakfast drink
1 cup instant tea

½ cup lemonade crystals
1 tablespoon cinnamon
1 teaspoon cloves

Combine all the ingredients. Mix thoroughly. For individual servings, place 2 teaspoons (or more if desired) of the mix in a cup of hot water. Stir and serve very hot. Add spirits if you wish.

Makes about 6 cups of mix.

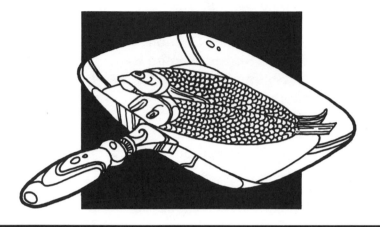

Seafood

Salmon

Sauce for Cold Poached Salmon

1 large Bermuda onion
2 green peppers
4 hard-boiled eggs
4 garlic dill pickles
1 quart mayonnaise
¼ cup horseradish

½ cup chili sauce
2 tablespoons capers
1 clove garlic, pressed
Salt & pepper
1 cup whipping cream,
   whipped

Grind or blend the onion with the green peppers, eggs, and pickles. Combine with the mayonnaise, horseradish, chili sauce, capers, garlic, and salt and pepper to taste. Blend well and fold in the whipped cream. Spread over the fish and decorate with sliced olives, radishes, cucumbers, etc. This sauce is enough for a 5 or 6 pound fish.

Serves 8 to 10.

Poaching Fish

Poaching is a method of cooking in a simmering liquid. In poaching, the fish are placed in a single layer in a shallow, wide pan, such as a large fry pan, and barely covered with liquid. The liquid used in poaching may be lightly salted water, water seasoned with herbs, milk, or a mixture of white wine and water, to name just a few. As with other methods of fish cookery, it is important not to overcook the fish. Simmer the fish in the liquid in a covered pan just until the fish flakes easily, usually 5-10 minutes. Because the poaching liquid contains flavorful juices, the liquid is often reduced and thickened to make a sauce for the fish.

Indian Salmon Barbecue, Patio Style

2 tablespoons salt
3 pound salmon fillet, skin on

¼ cup melted butter
½ teaspoon garlic salt
2 tablespoons lemon juice

Rub the salt evenly over all the surfaces of the fish several hours or the day before the barbecue. Keep cold. Prepare a bed of hot coals using either hardwood or charcoal. Place the fish in a well-greased double-hinged broiler. Turn the fish, flesh side down, fairly close to the coals until the surface is nicely browned. Turn flesh side up, and place far enough from the coals (about 10 inches) so that cooking will proceed at a moderate pace. Keep just enough wood on the fire so that smoke is slowly generated. During cooking, baste periodically with a mixture of melted butter, garlic salt, and lemon juice. The fish is done when it can be easily flaked with a fork. Cooking time depends on the temperature of the coals and the thickness of the fillet, but it is generally 10 minutes per inch of thickness of the fillet.

Serves 6 to 8.

Frank's Bell Island Italian Baked Salmon

2 medium onions, chopped
1 teaspoon sugar
½ cup olive oil, divided
2 cloves garlic, minced
1 tablespoon Italian seasoning

2 tablespoons chopped
 parsley
1 (2 pound) can tomato sauce
1 (tomato sauce) can of water
4-8 salmon fillets

Sauté the onions and sugar in ¼ cup olive oil until transparent. In a 2 quart saucepan, add the remaining olive oil and minced garlic. Sauté for 3 minutes over high heat, then add all the other ingredients and the sautéed onions. Simmer the sauce for 2 hours and then pour over the salmon fillets. For 4 fillets, use a 9x9x2-inch pan; for 8 fillets, a 13x9x2-inch pan. Cover the pan with heavy-duty foil. Bake at 350° for 30 minutes.

Serves 4 to 8.

Gravlax (Marinated Salmon)

1 (10 pound) salmon
1 cup olive oil
1 cup salt
1 cup brown sugar
Pinch of saltpeter

1 tablespoon white pepper
1 tablespoon ground allspice
1 teaspoon mace
¼ cup fresh, chopped dill or
   2 tablespoons dill weed

Clean, scale, and wash the salmon thoroughly. Then split it lengthwise, removing the backbone, or fillet, removing all the bones. Rinse the fillets, drain, and wipe dry. Rub the olive oil well into both sides of the fish halves. Mix together the salt, brown sugar, saltpeter (this is for a bright red color), white pepper, ground allspice, and mace. Coat both fillets on the cut side with the seasoning mixture, rubbing into the flesh. Place the fresh, chopped dill or dill weed on both sides. Place both halves together, with the cut sides together. Reshape the sides. Set in a shallow pan and press under moderate weight for 48 hours. Liquid will drain from the fish. Be sure the pan is large enough to allow for drainage. Serve thinly sliced. The fish may be packaged in glass. Store at 34° to 40°. It can be held for several weeks. Serve as an hors d'ouevre, cold with salad, on open-faced sandwiches, or as part of a buffet.

Seattle Salmon Supreme

1 (8-10 pound) salmon,
   dressed and cleaned
1 cup dairy sour cream
1 small cucumber,
   seeded & diced
½ cup sliced pimento-
   stuffed olives
1 teaspoon lemon peel
1 teaspoon snipped parsley

1 teaspoon nutmeg
1 teaspoon salt
¼ cup butter
2 tablespoons flour
½ cup water
¼ cup honey
¼ cup lemon juice
1 teaspoon instant
   chicken bouillon

Lay the salmon on a large sheet of heavy aluminum foil on a shallow baking pan. Combine the sour cream, cucumber, olives, lemon peel, parsley, nutmeg, and salt; spread in the cavity. Wrap up the entire salmon with foil. Bake at 350° for about 1½ hours or until the fish flakes easily with a fork. Set the salmon on a large platter and remove the skin. Spread the following glaze over the fish: melt the butter in a saucepan, blend in the flour, and add the remaining ingredients. Cook, stirring constantly, until thickened and clear. Cool.

Serves 8 to 12.

Baked Stuffed Salmon with Shrimp Sauce

1 cup finely minced celery
⅓ cup finely minced onion
2 tablespoons butter
¾ cup fine, dry bread crumbs
2 eggs
1 teaspoon salt
¼ teaspoon pepper
Juice of ½ lemon

2 tablespoons Sauterne
8-10 oysters, shelled
3-4 pound salmon fillet,
   (⅔ pound per person)
6-8 crab legs
2-3 cups medium White
   Sauce (see index)
¾ cup cooked shrimp

Sauté the celery and onion in melted butter. Mix in a bowl the bread crumbs, eggs, salt, pepper, lemon juice, and Sauterne. Add the sautéed vegetables to complete the dressing. Place the oysters down the center of the fillet. Cover with dressing. Place the crab legs along

40

side of the dressing. Fold the edges of the fillet together; place seam side down in the bottom of the pan. Add a little butter and seasonings on top. Cover the pan with foil. Bake at 350° for 1 hour. Mix the shrimp with the medium white sauce. Add a little crab meat or minced clams, if desired. Pour over the individual slices of stuffed salmon.

Serves 6 to 8.

Baked Stuffed Salmon

1 (3-4 pound) salmon, dressed
1 ½ teaspoons salt
3 slices bacon

Bread Stuffing:
3 tablespoons chopped
*   onion*

¾ cup chopped celery
6 tablespoons butter or
*   other fat, melted*
1 teaspoon salt
Dash pepper
1 teaspoon thyme, sage, or
*   savory seasoning*
1 quart day-old bread crumbs

Clean, scale, rinse, and pat dry the salmon. Sprinkle inside and out with salt. Stuff (with **Bread Stuffing**) the fish loosely; sew the opening with a needle and string or close with skewers. Place the fish in a well-greased baking pan. Arrange the bacon slices on the fish and bake at 350° for 40-60 minutes or until the fish flakes easily from the bone when tested with a fork. If the fish seems dry while baking, baste it occasionally with the dripping or with melted fat. Remove the strings or skewers, and serve immediately on a hot platter, plain or with a sauce.

Bread Stuffing: Cook the onion and celery in fat for about 10 minutes or until tender. Add the cooked vegetables and seasonings to the bread crumbs and mix thoroughly. If the dressing seems very dry, add 2 tablespoons of water, milk, or fish stock to moisten.

Barbecued Salmon

3-4 pounds salmon
Salt
2 tablespoons chopped
  onion
1 tablespoon butter or
  margarine

1 cup catsup
2 tablespoons vinegar
¼ cup lemon juice
3 tablespoons Worcestershire
  sauce
2 tablespoons brown sugar
Dash pepper

Place the salmon in a greased, shallow pan and sprinkle with salt. Lightly brown the onion in butter or margarine. Add the catsup, vinegar, lemon juice, Worcestershire sauce, brown sugar, ½ teaspoon salt, and pepper. Simmer 5 minutes and pour over the fish. Bake at 350° for 45-50 minutes, depending on the thickness of the salmon.

Serves 6 to 8.

Baked Salmon with Sour Cream Sauce

4 salmon fillets or steaks,
  serving size
1 tablespoon instant minced
  onion or 3 tablespoons
  fresh minced onion
1 tablespoon parsley flakes
Salt & pepper

1 cup dry white table wine
1 cup dairy sour cream
½ teaspoon dill weed
½ teaspoon dry shredded
  green onions or 2 tablespoons fresh green onions
Paprika

Arrange the salmon in a single layer in a greased, shallow baking dish. Sprinkle with onion, parsley, and salt and pepper. Pour the wine over the fish. Bake, uncovered, for 15 minutes at 375°. Remove the dish from the oven. Carefully pour off the liquid. Mix the sour cream, dill weed, green onions, and salt to taste. Spread over the salmon. Sprinkle with paprika. Return to the oven for 10 minutes or until the fish flakes when tested with a fork.

Serves 4.

Salmon and Shrimp

4 salmon steaks or fillets
½ cup dry, white wine
1 bay leaf
1 teaspoon onion powder
½ teaspoon salt
¼ teaspoon white pepper

Shrimp Sauce:
2 tablespoons butter
2 tablespoons flour
1 cup fish stock or
  chicken bouillon
1 (8 ounce) package frozen
  cooked & peeled
  Alaska shrimp
2 tablespoons dry sherry or
  cream

Rinse and dry the salmon steaks or fillets. Place them in a buttered 11½x7½x 1½-inch baking dish. Do not overlap the fish. Pour wine over the fish. Add a small piece of bay leaf, onion powder, salt, and white pepper. Cover the dish with foil, turning edges down to form a cover. Bake at 350° for 25 minutes or until the fish is done. While the fish is cooking, prepare the sauce.

Shrimp Sauce: Melt the butter and add the flour, stirring well. Add the fish stock or chicken bouillon and cook until thickened. Add the shrimp. Heat through and add the dry sherry or cream. Thin to desired consistency. Serve over salmon.

Serves 4.

Tuna

Easy Casserole

1 cup broken noodles
1 (6½ ounce) can tuna,
  drained & flaked
1½ cups shredded cheddar
  cheese
2 eggs
1 (13 ounce) can evaporated
  milk

2 teaspoons minced onion
½ teaspoon dry mustard
½ teaspoon salt
Dash pepper
¼ teaspoon paprika
1 tablespoon pimento,
  chopped

Cook the noodles in boiling salted water until tender. Alternate layers of noodles, tuna, and 1 cup cheddar cheese. Beat the eggs slightly and add the evaporated milk and seasonings. Pour over the noodles. Sprinkle the remainder of the cheese over the top. Bake at 350° for about 40 minutes.

Serves 4 to 6.

Fish & Field Casserole

1½ cups cooked vegetables
  (zucchini, cauliflower,
  broccoli, etc.)
4 ounces canned tuna,
  drained & flaked
⅔ cup skim milk ricotta
  cheese

1 medium tomato,
  peeled & chopped
½ cup finely chopped celery
¼ medium green pepper,
  chopped
⅛ teaspoon salt
Pepper to taste

Divide the vegetables evenly into 2 (10-inch) oven-proof dishes. Combine the remaining ingredients in a bowl. Divide the mixture evenly into 2 portions. Spread each portion over the vegetables. Bake at 350° for 10 minutes or until heated through.

Variation: Other fish or chicken may be used in place of tuna.

Serves 2.

Lemony Tuna Stroganoff

4 green onions, cut in 1-inch
    pieces (about ½ cup)
1 medium clove garlic,
    minced
2 tablespoons butter or
    margarine
1 (10¾ ounces) can cream of
    mushroom soup, undiluted
⅔ cup plain yogurt
⅓ cup milk
Grated peel and juice
    of ½ fresh lemon

Generous dash pepper
2 (7 ounce) cans tuna,
    drained & flaked
1 (4 ounce) can sliced
    mushrooms, drained
    (optional)
Hot cooked noodles or rice
Paprika
Lemon wedges (optional)
Parsley (optional)

In a skillet, sauté the green onions and garlic in butter until tender. Add the soup, yogurt, milk, lemon peel and juice, and pepper. Stir in the tuna and mushrooms; heat. Serve over hot cooked noodles or rice. Sprinkle with paprika. Garnish with lemon wedges and parsley, if desired.

Serves 4.

Tuna Casserole

3 cups fresh bread cubes
½ cup chopped green pepper
¼ cup chopped parsley
1 tablespoon finely chopped
    onion
⅛ teaspoon thyme
¼ cup butter
3 tablespoons flour
½ teaspoon salt

¼ teaspoon dry mustard
⅛ teaspoon white pepper
1½ cups milk
½ teaspoon Worcestershire
    sauce
2 (7¾ ounce) cans tuna
2 tablespoons lemon juice
Paprika
Egg slices (optional)
Parsley (optional)

In a bowl, lightly toss together the bread cubes, green pepper, parsley, onion, and thyme. Place in the bottom of a buttered, shallow 1½ quart casserole. In a 1 quart saucepan, melt the butter, stir in the flour, salt, dry mustard, and white pepper. Remove from the heat; gradually stir in the milk. Cook over medium heat, stirring constantly, until thickened. Cook, 2 additional minutes. Stir in the Worcestershire sauce. Place the tuna, flaked, on the bread mixture in the casserole. Sprinkle with lemon juice. Pour the sauce over all; sprinkle with paprika. Bake at 375° for 25-30 minutes. Garnish with egg slices and parsley, if desired.

Serves 6.

Tuna Rice Verde

2 (6½ ounce) cans chunk
   light tuna*
1 cup uncooked long-grain
   regular rice
2 tablespoons vegetable oil
1 cup chopped green onion
1 cup diced celery
1 cup chopped parsley

1 clove garlic, pressed
1 cube chicken bouillon
2 cups water
2 medium tomatoes,
   seeded & chopped**
2 teaspoons sweet basil,
   crumbled
½ teaspoon salt

Drain the tuna. In a skillet, brown the rice in oil. Meanwhile, combine the onion, celery, parsley, garlic, and bouillon cube with 1 cup water in a blender. Whir until smooth. Pour into the browned rice along with the remaining 1 cup water, tomatoes, basil, and salt. Cover; simmer 25 minutes. Stir in the tuna.

If the tuna is packed in oil, the oil may be used to replace the vegetable oil.

***1 pound can of tomatoes may be used instead of fresh tomatoes. Reduce water to 1 cup. Add more water if necessary.*

Serves 4.

Katherine's Tuna Bake

1 (20 pound) fresh tuna,
   filleted
2 quarts buttermilk
1 egg
½ cup water

Cracker crumbs
Seasoned onion salt
Dash garlic salt
½ cup butter

Place the fillets from the tuna in a large stainless steel, Pyrex, or plastic bowl. Cover with buttermilk. Soak for 12-24 hours. Remove 1 fillet, wipe free of buttermilk, and dry. Beat the egg and water (this amount is enough for 2 fillets). Cut the fillets in half, dip in beaten egg and water, then roll in the seasoned cracker crumbs. Allow to stand 30 minutes to set. Place half the butter in a 15x10½x1-inch baking dish, and then melt it in a 425° oven. Place the 2 halves of fillets in the butter and roll to coat. Melt the rest of the butter and baste the fish during baking. Bake at 425° for 10 minutes per inch of fish depth. Slice in 1-inch slices and serve hot with tartar or fish sauce.

Serves 8 to 10 with each fillet.

Tuna Orientale

1 (9¼ ounce) can tuna,
   drained
1 (10½ ounce) can cream
   of mushroom soup,
   undiluted
2 cups chow mein noodles

1 (8½ ounce) can pineapple
   tidbits, drained
1 cup dairy sour cream
½ cup chopped celery
¾ cup chopped cashews
2 tablespoons chopped
   pimento

In a large bowl, combine the tuna, soup, 1½ cups noodles, pineapple tidbits, sour cream, celery, ½ cup cashews, and pimento. Turn into a buttered 1 quart casserole. Garnish with the remaining noodles and cashews. Bake at 350° for 30-35 minutes.

Serves 6 to 8.

Pinchpenny Tuna-Egg Patties

White Sauce:
¼ cup butter or margarine
¼ cup flour
¼ teaspoon salt
⅛ teaspoon pepper
1 cup milk

4 hard-boiled eggs, chopped
1 (6½ ounce) can tuna,
    drained & flaked
3 tablespoons chopped
    pimento

2 tablespoons chopped onion
1 tablespoon snipped parsley
½ teaspoon celery salt
½ teaspoon paprika
Flour
2 eggs
2 tablespoons water
3 cups finely crushed corn
    flakes
1 tablespoon shortening
1 cup chili sauce

White Sauce: Melt the butter or margarine in a saucepan over low heat. Blend in the flour, salt, and pepper. Cook over low heat, stirring constantly, until the mixture is smooth and bubbly. Remove from heat. Stir in the milk. Heat to boiling, stirring constantly. Boil and stir 1 minute. Remove from heat.

Stir into the prepared **White Sauce**, the hard-boiled eggs, tuna, pimento, onion, parsley, celery salt, and paprika. Spread mixture in a greased 8x8x2-inch baking dish. Refrigerate one hour. Cut the tuna mixture into 9 squares. Coat the squares with flour; shape into patties. Beat the eggs and water slightly. Dip the patties into the egg mixture. Coat with the cereal crumbs. Melt the shortening in a skillet. Lightly brown the patties over low heat for about 5 minutes on each side. Heat the chili sauce in a saucepan over low heat. Serve the patties with warm chili sauce.

Serves 5 to 6.

White Fish

Gourmet Fish Sauce

3 pounds fresh cod or
   other white fish
6-8 bunches of leaves
   from celery tops
2 tablespoons lemon juice
2 small bay leaves
6 sprigs parsley
1 teaspoon salt
8 large onions, chopped
1 pound mushrooms, sliced
1 cup butter or margarine

½ pound fresh seedless
   grapes
½ cup flour
2 cups fish stock, reserved
1⅔ cups (1 large can)
   evaporated milk
¼ teaspoon marjoram
¼ teaspoon thyme, crushed
   to a powder
¼ cup chopped parsley
Steamed rice

Place the fresh fish, leaves from celery tops, lemon juice, bay leaves, parsley sprigs, and salt in a large saucepan. Add enough water to cover ingredients. (You will need 2 cups of this fish stock for the sauce.) Cover and simmer gently (do not boil) about 12-15 minutes or until the fish flakes. Let the fish stand in the stock until ready to combine with the sauce.

While the fish is poaching, sauté the onions and mushrooms in ½ cup butter or margarine. Stir frequently. When the mushrooms and onions have cooked down, add the fresh seedless grapes, and cook for about 5 minutes or until the grapes lighten in color and have heated through.

Prepare the cream sauce by melting ½ cup butter and adding the flour; stir and mix well. Add the fish stock, evaporated milk, marjoram, thyme, and parsley. Add the flaked fish (removing any bones), and combine with the onion, mushrooms, and green grapes. Check for seasonings. Heat and serve with steamed rice.

Serves 6.

Poached Sole with Sauce Mornay

4 pounds small sole fillets
½ sliced onion
1 lemon, thinly sliced
2 bay leaves, broken
½ teaspoon salt

Sauce Mornay:
1 tablespoon butter

1 tablespoon flour
1 cup half & half or cream
3 tablespoons grated Swiss
  or Gruyère cheese
2 tablespoons dry vermouth
Salt & pepper
Prawn or cocktail shrimp
Fresh parsley

Take the sole fillets and roll tightly with the dark side in the center. Place the rolls loosely, as rolled, into a low baking dish. Cover with water to the top of the sole only. Sprinkle the onion, lemon, bay leaves, and salt over the top. Cover the dish with foil or a lid and bake at 400° for 35-40 minutes. Check for doneness by making sure all the transparency is gone from the center of one of the larger rolls. The sole may be left uncovered in the pan until ready to serve. Remove with a slotted spoon and serve with **Sauce Mornay.**

Sauce Mornay: Melt the butter in heavy saucepan over low heat. Stir in the flour, cooking and stirring for 2-3 minutes. Heat the half and half or cream and stir slowly into the butter-flour mixture. Add the cheese. Cook over low heat until the cheese is barely melted. Add the vermouth and season with salt and pepper to taste. If the sauce appears too thick, a small amount of stock in which the fish was poached may be added. To serve, ladle the sauce over the rolled sole filets. Garnish with prawn or cocktail shrimp and fresh chopped parsley.

Serves 6.

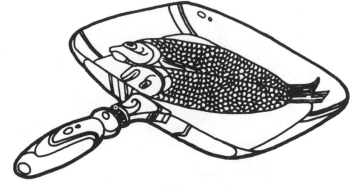

Poached Sole with Herb Cream Sauce

¼ cup butter
½ cup dry white wine
1 ½ pounds sole fillets
½ teaspoon salt
Few dashes pepper
¼ cup chopped parsley

Herb Cream Sauce:
1 tablespoon vinegar

1 ½ teaspoons steak sauce
½ teaspoon thyme
½ teaspoon oregano
2 tablespoons minced
    green onion
Few dashes pepper
2 egg yolks
½ cup hot melted butter
½ cup whipping cream,
    whipped

Put the butter and wine in a baking dish and heat in at 400° for 5 minutes or until the butter melts. Meanwhile, lay the fish fillets flat; sprinkle with salt, pepper, and parsley. Roll up, turn in wine butter sauce to coat, and place seam side down in a baking dish. Cover tightly. Bake at 400° for 25 minutes or until cooked through. Serve with **Herb Cream Sauce.**

Herb Cream Sauce: Combine the vinegar, steak sauce, thyme, oregano, green onion, pepper and egg yolks in a blender. Whir until smooth. Gradually blend in the hot melted butter. Cool. Fold in the whipped cream before serving.

Makes 1⅔ cups sauce, for 4 to 6 servings.

East-West Baked Sole

Juice of ½ lemon
1 avocado, sliced
1 banana, sliced
1 pound sole or other
   white fish fillets
Salt & pepper
2 cups cooked rice

2 tablespoons sliced
   green onion
½ teaspoon curry powder
½ fresh lemon, sliced in
   cartwheels
¼ cup butter or margarine,
   melted

To prevent darkening, sprinkle lemon juice on the avocado and banana slices. Arrange the fillets in a 13x9x2-inch baking dish; sprinkle with salt and pepper. Combine the rice, onion, and curry powder; mix well. Spoon the rice mixture over the fillets. Arrange the following alternately over the rice: the lemon cartwheels, avocado, and banana slices. Sprinkle with butter. Cover with foil; bake at 350° for 20 minutes or until the fish flakes easily with a fork.

Serves 4.

Fish Baked in Wine

2 pounds fish fillets or slices*
Salt & pepper
1 large onion, sliced
1 cup white table wine
3 tablespoons butter
   or margarine

1 small can tomato sauce or
   2 fresh tomatoes, sliced
½ green pepper, sliced
2 teaspoons Worcestershire
   sauce

Sprinkle the fish with salt and pepper; cover with the sliced onion. Pour wine over all and let it stand for 30 minutes. Melt the butter in a large, shallow baking pan; remove the fish and onion from the wine and place in the pan. Cover with the tomatoes and green pepper; sprinkle with salt. Bake at 375° for about 35 minutes or until the fish flakes, basting it frequently with the wine in which the fish was soaked mixed with the Worcestershire sauce.

*Any white fish (sole, halibut, sea bass, etc.,) or salmon is good prepared this way.

Serves 4 to 6.

Baked Sole with Mushrooms

8 fillets of sole*
1 cup sour cream
1 (10¾ ounce) can cream of
mushroom soup, undiluted

½ cup dry white wine
or ½ cup club soda
1 (4 ounce) can mushrooms
& liquid or about 10
fresh mushrooms

Rinse and pat dry the fillets of sole. Roll up each fillet and place in a baking dish. Mix together the rest of the ingredients, and pour over the fillets. Bake at 350° for approximately 30 minutes or until the fish flakes.

*Red snapper may be substituted for sole.

Serves 4.

Washington Baked Fish Fillets

2 pounds flounder fillets or
other fresh or frozen fish
½ cup flour
1 teaspoon salt
Dash pepper
¼ cup roasted, diced almonds

1 tablespoon grated
lemon rind
¼ cup lemon juice
¼ cup melted fat or oil
¼ cup chopped chives
Lemon wedges
Parsley

Thaw the frozen fillets or use the fresh fillets; skin if necessary. Cut into serving-size portions. Combine the flour, salt, and pepper. Roll the fish in the flour mixture. Place the fish in a well-greased, shallow baking dish. Combine the almonds, lemon rind, lemon juice, and fat; mix well. Pour over the fish. Bake at 350° for 25-30 minutes, or until the fish flakes easily when tested with a fork. Sprinkle chives over the top of the fish. Garnish with lemon wedges and parsley.

Serves 6.

Halibut with Rice & Vegetables

3 tablespoons fat
¾ cup chopped onions
2 cups grated raw potatoes
1 cup grated raw carrots
1 cup cooked rice
1 cup chopped celery

2 cups raw cubed halibut
2 cups canned tomatoes
1 teaspoon salt
¼ teaspoon pepper
½ cup dry bread crumbs
2 tablespoons butter

Melt the fat, add the onions, and cook until clear. In a greased casserole, arrange alternate layers of raw potatoes, carrots, cooked rice, celery, fish, tomatoes, and cooked onions. Season each layer with salt and pepper; add boiling water to barely cover the vegetables. Sprinkle the top with crumbs and dot with butter. Bake, uncovered, at 375° for 1 hour.

Halibut in Sour Cream

1-1½ pounds halibut
  (4 slices)
2 tablespoons lemon juice
2 tablespoons butter

½ teaspoon salt
½ teaspoon tarragon, crushed
2 tablespoons minced onion
1 cup dairy sour cream
½ cup grated cheddar cheese

Pat dry the halibut, then brush with lemon juice. Melt the butter in a skillet. Place the halibut in the skillet. Combine the salt, tarragon leaves, minced onion, and dairy sour cream, then pour over the halibut. Cover and cook over low heat about 25 minutes or until the fish flakes. Simmer, but do not boil. Just before serving, sprinkle with grated cheddar cheese.

Serves 4.

Halibut Creole

2 pounds North Pacific
   halibut
½ cup chopped onion
¼ cup chopped green pepper
1 clove garlic, minced
2 tablespoons oil
1 (15 ounce) can tomato
   sauce

1 tablespoon chopped parsley
1 ½ teaspoons oregano
1 ½ teaspoons Worcestershire
   sauce
1 teaspoon salt
⅛ teaspoon pepper
2 teaspoons sugar

Cut the halibut into 1-inch chunks, discarding the skin and bones. Set aside. Sauté the onion, green pepper, and garlic in oil until tender. Add the remaining ingredients. Simmer, uncovered, about 20 minutes. Meanwhile, place the halibut chunks on an oiled broiling pan. Broil, turning once, until the halibut flakes when tested with a fork, about 5 minutes. Before serving, add the halibut to the sauce and heat gently.

This recipe comes from the Halibut Association of North America.

Makes 4 to 6 main dish servings or 12 appetizer servings.

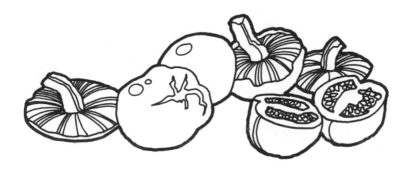

Clams

Clams Oregano

½ cup butter
4 cloves garlic, mashed
¼ cup fine bread crumbs
1 teaspoon oregano, crushed
Hot pepper sauce

1 teaspoon finely chopped
    fresh parsley
2 tablespoons minced onion
3 dozen littleneck or
    butter clams

Combine the butter, mashed garlic, bread crumbs, crushed oregano, a few dashes of hot pepper sauce, parsley, and onion; mix well. Place one teaspoon of this mixture on top of each littleneck or butter clam on the half shell. These may be refrigerated for one day and still be excellent. They can be frozen and kept for 2 weeks. When ready to serve, bake at 375° for 10 minutes, then brown under the broiler.

Makes 36.

Baked Clam au Gratin

2 cups clams,
    coarsely ground
2 eggs
½ cup plus 2 tablespoons
    grated cheddar cheese
1 teaspoon salt
½ teaspoon white pepper
½ cup dry sherry

½ cup butter
3 strips bacon, diced
⅓ cup chopped celery
⅓ cup chopped green pepper
⅓ cup chopped green onion
½ cup sifted flour⁻
2 cups milk
Paprika

Mix together the clams with the eggs, ½ cup cheddar cheese, salt, pepper, and sherry. Set aside. In a large frying pan, place the butter, bacon, celery, green pepper, and green onion. Braise slowly, but do not brown. Blend in the flour and cook slowly for 2 minutes. Gradually add the milk, stirring until smooth and thickened. Stir in the clam mixture. Transfer to a buttered baking dish and sprinkle with 2 tablespoons grated cheddar cheese. Dust with paprika. Bake at 350° for 10-15 minutes, or until hot and nicely browned on top.

Serves 4 to 6.

Artichoke-Clam Casserole

1 (6 ounce) jar marinated
  artichoke hearts
½ cup chopped onion
¼ cup flour
1 (6½ ounce) can minced
  clams (or fresh equivalent)
¾ cup milk (approximately)

1 teaspoon mustard
4 teaspoons chopped parsley
3 tablespoons butter
¾ cup bread crumbs
Cherry tomatoes
Lemon wedges

Drain the oil from the artichoke hearts into a pan. Sauté the onions in the oil. Blend in the flour. Drain the minced clams and put the nectar in a measuring cup. Add enough milk to measure 1¼ cups liquid. Stir into the onion to make a thick cream sauce. Add the mustard, 1 teaspoon parsley, and clams to the sauce. Cut the artichoke hearts in halves and place in a buttered 1½ quart casserole. Cover with the creamy clam mixture. Melt the butter. Add the bread crumbs and 1 tablespoon chopped parsley. Sprinkle the crumb mixture over the clams. Bake at 400° for 20 minutes. Garnish with cherry tomatoes and lemon wedges.

Serves 4.

Fried Clams

6 pounds shell clams or
  1½ pints shucked clams
¾ teaspoon salt
⅛ teaspoon pepper

1 egg
1 tablespoon milk
1 cup bread crumbs
Melted fat

Shuck the shell clams. Wash the meats to remove any sand. Remove the dark body portion and the tip of the siphon. Drain and sprinkle with salt and pepper. Beat the egg slightly and add the milk, blending it in. Dip the clams in the egg and roll in the bread crumbs. Place the clams in a heavy frying pan which contains about ⅛ inch of melted fat, hot but not smoking. Fry at moderate heat. When the clams are brown on one side, turn carefully and brown on the other side. Serve immediately on a hot platter, plain or with a sauce.

Note: If the clams are large, the siphon may be removed and ground for use in chowder.

Serves 6.

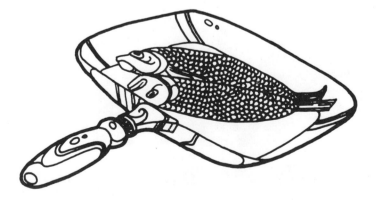

Crab

Company Crab

1 (6 ounce) package Alaska
   King crabmeat, frozen
¼ cup butter or margarine
1 cup sliced mushrooms
3 tablespoons flour
1¾ cups half & half
½ teaspoon salt

2 egg yolks
½ cup sour cream
2 tablespoons sherry
Dash nutmeg
Hot cooked rice, noodles, or
   patty shells

Thaw and drain the crabmeat; save the liquid. Melt the butter in a saucepan. Add the mushrooms and sauté until tender. Stir in the flour until smooth. Add the half and half, crab liquid, and salt. Cook until thickened. Beat the egg yolks into the sour cream and stir in ½ cup of the hot mixture. Return to the remaining hot liquid and continue to cook over low heat for 3-4 minutes. Stir in the crabmeat, sherry, and nutmeg. Serve over rice, noodles, or patty shells.

Serves 4.

Crab Foo Yung

8 eggs, beaten
1 teaspoon salt
¼ teaspoon pepper
1 cup minced onions
1 cup sliced celery

½ cup minced green pepper
1 teaspoon soy sauce
2 cans snow crab
4 tablespoons peanut oil
2-3 tablespoons finely sliced
   green onion

Combine the eggs, salt, pepper, onion, celery, green pepper, soy sauce, and snow crab. Place the peanut oil in a skillet. Heat to frying temperature (375°) and drop the mixture by tablespoons to patty size. Fry until golden. Turn and fry on the other side. Place on a warm platter. Serve with finely sliced green onions sprinkled on top.

Serves 6 to 8.

Crab Casserole

1 (6½ ounce) can snow crab
½ cup mayonnaise
1 tablespoon chili sauce
1 teaspoon red wine vinegar
1 teaspoon celery salt

½ teaspoon prepared mustard
1 avocado, diced
2 cups hot cooked rice
2 tablespoons grated
  Parmesan cheese

Mix together the first six ingredients. Fold in the avocado. Heat just to warm, do not cook, and pour over the hot rice. Top with Parmesan cheese. Place under the broiler and broil until the cheese melts.

Variation: Serve over Chinese noodles, egg noodles or toast. Little green peas may be added for variety. Tuna, salmon, crab, or shrimp may be used instead of snow crab.

Serves 4.

Crab-Spinach Soufflé

¼ cup flour
1 teaspoon salt
¼ cup oil
1 cup milk, scalded
1 teaspoon Worcestershire
  sauce
⅛ teaspoon Tabasco sauce

4 eggs, separated
1 cup chopped, cooked, fresh
  or frozen spinach,
  well drained
1 cup finely flaked crab meat
¼ cup grated cheese

Blend the flour and salt into the oil in a medium-size saucepan. Slowly stir in the milk, Worcestershire sauce, and Tabasco sauce. Cook, stirring constantly, until the mixture is thick; cool. Beat the egg whites just until they form soft peaks in a medium-size bowl. Beat the egg yolks until cream-thick in a large bowl; blend in the cooled sauce, chopped spinach, and crab meat. Fold in the beaten egg whites. Spoon into 8 (6 ounce) custard cups or individual soufflé dishes. Set the cups in a large shallow pan for easy handling. Bake at 400° for 20 minutes or until puffy, firm, and golden. Sprinkle grated cheese over the top.

Makes 8 servings.

Quick Crab Quiche

1 (6 ounce) package frozen
  crabmeat, thawed, or
  1 (6½ ounce) can crabmeat
½ cup shredded Swiss or
  cheddar cheese
1 (9-inch) unbaked pie shell
6 eggs
1 ½ cups half & half,
  light cream, or milk

1 tablespoon instant
  minced onion
1 tablespoon dry white
  wine (optional)
½ teaspoon salt
½ teaspoon dry mustard
½ teaspoon dried tarragon
  leaves, crushed

Drain the crabmeat (use liquid to replace part of the 1 ½ cups half and half, if desired), and flake. Sprinkle the crabmeat and cheese into the pie shell. Beat together the remaining ingredients until combined. Pour over the crabmeat and cheese. Bake at 375° for 30-35 minutes or until a knife inserted near center comes out clean. Let stand 5 minutes before serving.

To Microwave: In a 1 quart measure or medium mixing bowl, stir together the half and half, onion, wine, and seasonings. Microwave 2 minutes on *HIGH*. Stir in the crabmeat and cheese. Microwave an additional 2 minutes on *HIGH*. Stir until the cheese is melted, about 1 minute. Beat the eggs until well blended. Gradually stir in the hot mixture until thoroughly blended. Pour into a pie shell in a glass pie plate. Microwave 18 minutes on *DEFROST*, rotating the dish ¼ turn every 3 minutes, or until a knife inserted halfway between center and edge comes out clean. Let stand 10 minutes.

Seafood Asparagus Divan/Microwave

2 (8 ounce) packages frozen
  cut asparagus or 1 pound
  fresh asparagus
1 (7½ ounce) can crab meat,
  drained & flaked
1 cup shelled, cooked shrimp
  or 1 (4½ ounce) can
  medium shrimp, drained

3 hard-boiled eggs, sliced
2 packages (1⅛ ounce)
  hollandaise sauce mix
1½ cups milk
½ cup dairy sour cream
1 tablespoon grated
  Parmesan cheese

If you use fresh asparagus, wash and cut off the tough ends. Leave whole or cut the spears into 3 to 4-inch lengths. Cook in a 2 quart covered casserole with ¼ cup water. Rearrange once. Cook 7-8 minutes. For frozen asparagus, place cartons side by side in a 10x6x1½-inch baking dish. Make a small slit through the top of each carton. Cook at *HIGH* for 13 minutes; drain well. Layer the asparagus, crabmeat (all cartilage removed), and shrimp in the dish. Top with the egg slices. Cook, covered, at *HIGH* for 7 minutes, until heated through. Cover and keep warm. In 4-cup glass measure, combine the hollandaise sauce mix and milk. Cook, uncovered, at *HIGH* for 4 minutes, or until the mixture boils, stirring after each minute. Stir in the sour cream; spoon over the casserole. Top with cheese. Serve immediately.

Serves 6.

Seafood Soufflé

4 slices bread, buttered
1 (7½ ounce) can snow crab
1½-2 cups grated American
  cheese

3 eggs
1½ cups milk
1½ teaspoons salt
1 teaspoon dry mustard
Paprika

Cut the bread, crusts removed, into 1-inch cubes. Cover the bottom of a greased casserole with alternate layers of bread, snow crab, and grated cheese until all is used. Beat the eggs with milk, salt, and dry mustard. Pour over the casserole. Sprinkle with paprika. Bake at 350° for 40-45 minutes. The soufflé may chill overnight before baking.

Serves 6 to 8.

Samish Bay Crab Louis

½ cup mayonnaise
3 tablespoons French
   dressing
2 tablespoons chili sauce
1 tablespoon snipped chives
   or freeze-dried chives
½ teaspoon horseradish
½ teaspoon Worcestershire
   sauce

Salt & pepper to taste
2 (6½ ounce) cans crab meat
1 head lettuce
3 hard-boiled eggs
Tomato wedges
Pickles
1 tablespoon chopped
   green olives

Combine the dressings and seasonings. Add the crab meat. Check seasonings. Prepare the lettuce for 6 salads. Spoon the dressing over the lettuce. Garnish with hard-boiled eggs, tomato wedges, pickles, and green olives.

Serves 6.

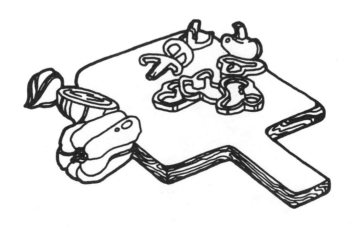

Oysters

Oysters with Spinach Noodles

6 ounces spinach noodles
3 cups water
1 teaspoon salt
1 teaspoon olive oil
1 cup freshly grated
Parmesan cheese
1 (6½ ounce) minced clams,
drained
1 (4 ounce) can mushrooms,
pieces & stems, drained
3 tablespoons minced
green pepper

Pinch dry thyme, crushed
1 (10 ounce) jar extra small
Pacific oysters
¼ cup dry sherry
2 slices cooked & crumbled
bacon
½ teaspoon paprika
½ teaspoon garlic salt
Pinch turmeric (optional)
Cocktail sauce
Lemon wedges

Cook the noodles in boiling water with salt and olive oil, 7-10 minutes, or until they are *al dente*. Drain and transfer to a bowl and add ½ cup Parmesan cheese, the minced clams, mushrooms, green pepper, and thyme. Combine and transfer to a flameproof, well-buttered baking dish, 11¾x7½x 1¾-inches. Top with the oysters, sprinkle with ½ cup Parmesan cheese, the sherry, crumbled bacon, and seasonings. Broil, about 5 inches from the heat, for 3 minutes; then bake, covered with foil, at 400° for 10 minutes. Serve with a cocktail sauce and lemon wedges.

Serves 4.

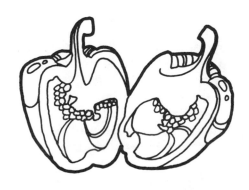

Oyster Pie

1⅔ cups saltine cracker
   crumbs
½ cup butter, softened
2 tablespoon water
1 onion, chopped
1 pint oysters, drained &
   chopped

1 can cream of mushroom
   soup, undiluted
3 eggs, beaten
¼ cup milk
½ cup grated cheddar
   cheese

Blend the cracker crumbs, ¼ cup butter, and water. Turn into 9-inch pie plate and press against the bottom and sides. Melt ¼ cup butter in a skillet and sauté the onion until lightly browned. Add the oysters and simmer for about 10 minutes. Add the soup. Blend in the beaten eggs and milk, along with the cheese. Pour into the crumb shell. Bake at 325° for 50-60 minutes. The pie may be allowed to stand for a short time before serving.

Serves 4 to 6.

Oysters Casino

30 medium-size oysters,
   in the shell
Rock salt
10 strips bacon
1 medium onion,
   finely chopped
½ green pepper,
   finely chopped

2 tablespoons butter
1 tablespoon canned
   pimento, chopped
½ teaspoon salt
¼ teaspoon pepper
⅛ teaspoon cayenne pepper
   (optional)
1 tablespoon lemon juice

Wash and rinse the oysters in the shell in cold water. Open or shuck the oysters or have them shucked at the store. Place the shells on a bed of rock salt in a shallow pan. (The salt keeps the oysters level so their juice does not spill.) Place the oysters in another shallow pan and heat in 350° oven for 5 minutes. Partially cook the bacon, which has been cut in thirds. Sauté the onion and green pepper in butter. Add the pimento, salt, pepper, and cayenne pepper. Add the lemon juice. Return the

70

oysters to the shells. Spoon the sauce mixture over each oyster. Top with the bacon. Place under the broiler and broil about 2-5 minutes, or until the bacon is crisp and the oysters are hot.

Serves 6.

Oysters O'Keefe

4 tablespoons butter
4 tablespoons flour
2 cups milk
1 teaspoon salt
¼ teaspoon pepper
⅛ teaspoon dry mustard
⅛ teaspoon curry powder
  (optional)
½ teaspoon Worcestershire
  sauce

1 cup grated sharp
  cheddar cheese
Juice of ½ lemon
  (1½ tablespoons)
1 (16 ounce) jar Willapa
  Pacific oysters & liquor
1 teaspoon grated lemon rind
8 slices dry toast
Paprika
Chopped parsley

Melt the butter in a saucepan and blend in the flour; gradually stir in the milk. Stir until the mixture thickens. Cook about 3 minutes longer. Add the seasonings. Add the cheese to the cream sauce. Keep the sauce warm. Squeeze the lemon juice into the oyster liquor, adding the lemon rind. Poach the oysters in liquor and lemon juice until the edges curl. Cut the toast into points. Cut the oysters into 3 or 4 pieces for each serving, place 4 toast points on a plate, and cover with the sauce. Place under the broiler and heat until bubbling. Garnish with extra toast points, grated cheese, paprika, and parsley.

Serves 4.

Shrimp

Alaska Shrimp

1 cup chopped onion
2 tablespoons butter
3 cups sliced celery
¾ cup chopped green pepper
1 (4 ounce) can mushroom
   pieces & stems
1 (8½ ounce) can water
   chestnuts, sliced
1 (4 ounce) jar pimentos,
   sliced
1 teaspoon salt

½ teaspoon celery salt
¼ teaspoon sweet basil,
   crushed
2 (8 ounce) packages Alaska
   frozen shrimp
1 (6 ounce) package cashews,
   chopped
2 (10½ ounce) cans cream of
   celery soup
2 (3 ounce) cans Chinese
   noodles

Sauté the onion in butter, adding the sliced celery and chopped green pepper. Stir and cook a few minutes. Add the mushrooms and liquid, water chestnuts, pimentos, salt, celery salt, basil, shrimp, cashews, and cream of celery soup. Heat to a simmering temperature. Place the Chinese noodles in a buttered 3½ quart casserole or other large baking dish. Cover with the shrimp mixture. Cover with a second can of Chinese noodles. Bake at 350° for 30 minutes or until hot and bubbly.

Serves 6 to 8.

Barbecued Shrimp

½ cup butter, melted
½ cup chopped onion
1 cup chopped celery
¼ cup chopped parsley
2 tablespoons lemon juice

3 cloves garlic, minced
1 teaspoon basil
1 teaspoon dry mustard
1 teaspoon salt
2 (6½ ounce) cans shrimp
Steamed rice

Combine the melted butter, onion, celery, parsley, lemon juice, garlic, basil, dry mustard, and salt. Add the shrimp. Simmer for 10 minutes. Serve over steamed rice.

Serves 4 to 6.

73

Prawns with Tomato Sauce

1 pound raw prawns
(size 12-20 or smaller)
1 ½ tablespoons oil
½ teaspoon salt
1 clove garlic, mashed
1 slice fresh ginger
(about the size of a quarter)

Tomato sauce:
2½ tablespoons oil

1 tablespoon fresh ginger,
slivered in strips
½ cup catsup
4 teaspoons granulated sugar
1 tablespoon sherry wine
½ cup water
1 teaspoon cornstarch,
mixed with
1 teaspoon water
⅓ cup green onions, cut
into 1-inch lengths

Shell, devein, and butterfly the prawns. (When you butterfly, cut almost all the way through.) Put the oil in a fry pan over high heat. When hot, add the salt, garlic, and ginger and brown lightly. Add the drained prawns and stir-fry over high heat for about 2 minutes. Remove the prawns to a bowl. Rinse out the fry pan and dry.

Tomato Sauce: Put the oil in a fry pan over medium heat. When the oil is hot, add the ginger and brown lightly. Ginger browns quickly. Add the catsup, sugar, sherry wine, and ½ cup water. Mix. Thicken with the cornstarch and water mixture. Add the drained, cooked prawns and green onions. Mix and stir-fry about ½ minute. Put in a serving dish. Serve with white rice.

Variations: Add ½ teaspoon curry with the catsup, or add a few drops of hot sauce.

Serves 3 to 4.

Spaghetti with Shellfish Sauce

3 cloves garlic, diced
½ cup Italian olive oil
5-6 squid, cleaned & sliced
2 (15 ounce) cans tomato
   sauce with tomato bits
2 teaspoons capers
8 small stuffed olives, diced
2 tablespoons minced parsley
1 teaspoon salt
¼ teaspoon lemon pepper
   seasoning

⅓ pound Alaska shrimp meat
1 (6 ounce) box frozen Alaska
   King crab
1 pound fresh clams, cleaned,
   or 1 (16 ounce) can
   baby clams
1 pound Italian spaghetti
Butter
Parmesan cheese

Sauté the garlic in olive oil; add the sliced squid and cook for 2-3 minutes. Add the tomato sauce, capers, stuffed olives, parsley, salt, and lemon pepper seasoning. Simmer gently for 5 minutes. Add the shrimp, crab, and clams. Stir and correct the seasoning. Cook gently for 15 minutes. While the sauce is simmering, cook the spaghetti in salted water. Drain, butter, and serve with shellfish sauce. Parmesan cheese may be served on the side for those who prefer a cheese flavor.

*Complete the meal with Italian French bread, tossed green salad, and ice cream with **Brandied Fruit** topping.*

Serves 6 to 8.

Stir Fried Shrimp and Vegetables

2 tablespoons peanut oil
1 teaspoon salt
2 cloves garlic, minced
10 ounces medium shrimp,
*   shelled, deveined,& halved*
1 cup Chinese mushrooms,
*   softened in water & cut*
*   into strips*
4 stalks bok choy, sliced
*   diagonally*
1 cup sliced bamboo shoots
¼ pound fresh sugar pea
*   pods, sliced diagonally*

½ cup sliced water chestnuts
2 teaspoons light soy sauce
1 teaspoon sherry
1 teaspoon sugar
½ teaspoon grated ginger
½ cup chicken stock

Thickening:
2 tablespoons cornstarch
1 teaspoon dark soy sauce
¼ teaspoon white pepper
3 tablespoons water

Heat the peanut oil until hot. Add the salt and minced garlic and stir-fry until browned. Add the shrimp and sauté until the shrimp starts to turn pink. Add the mushrooms, bok choy, bamboo shoots, pea pods, and water chestnuts; stir-fry for approximately 1 minute. Combine the soy sauce, sherry, sugar, grated ginger, and chicken stock. Add to the shrimp and vegetables and stir-fry for an additional 1-2 minutes.

Thickening: Mix the ingredients together; make a well in the center of the shrimp-vegetable mixture, and add the **Thickening.**   When the sauce thickens, mix well, and serve hot.

Serves 4.

Shrimp Cantonese with Rice

2 cups diagonally sliced
   celery
¼ pound onions, sliced
1 pound cooked shrimp,
   cut in half lengthwise
3 cups chopped spinach
   leaves
¼ pound Chinese pea pods

½ cup sliced water chestnuts
½ cup sliced bamboo shoots
1 ½ cups chicken stock
¼ cup soy sauce
2 tablespoons cornstarch
2 tablespoons water
¼ teaspoon pepper
2 cups cooked enriched rice

In a large nonstick skillet, brown the celery and onions. Add the shrimp, spinach, pea pods, water chestnuts, and bamboo shoots. Cover and cook 1 minute. In a small bowl combine the stock, soy sauce, cornstarch dissolved in water, and pepper. Stir into the shrimp-vegetable mixture. Cook, stirring until the sauce is thickened, about 2 minutes. Serve over hot rice.

Variation: For **Shrimp and Pork Cantonese:** *follow the basic recipe, but use 8 ounces cooked shrimp and 8 ounces cooked pork.*

Serves 4.

Avocado-Shrimp Curry

2 tablespoons butter or
  margarine
1½ teaspoons curry powder
1 teaspoon salt
½ cup chopped onion
1 (16 ounce) can stewed
  tomatoes

1 (8 ounce) package frozen
  Alaska shrimp
2 tablespoons lemon juice
1 cup dairy sour cream
3-4 avocados
Buttered rice
Chutney

Melt the butter in a saucepan. Add the curry powder and salt. Stir together and add the chopped onion. Sauté until clear. Add the stewed tomatoes and frozen shrimp. Bring to a simmer. Cook until the shrimp are heated through and thawed. Add the lemon juice and sour cream. Heat thoroughly, but do not boil. Cut the avocados in halves and remove the seed and skin. Fill the centers with the hot curry. Serve on a bed of buttered rice accompanied with chutney.

Serves 6 to 8.

Banana Shrimp Boat Casserole

2 tablespoons butter or
  margarine
¾ cup chopped onion
½ cup chopped green pepper
1 cup sliced celery
1 (8 ounce) package frozen,
  shelled, cooked shrimp
  (2 cups cooked, cleaned
  shrimp)

1 (10¾ ounce) can cream of
  mushroom soup
1 teaspoon salt
1 teaspoon chili powder
Fresh ground pepper to taste
3 cups cooked rice
2 bananas, peeled and diced

Heat the butter or margarine in a skillet and sauté the onion, green pepper, and celery for about 5 minutes. Stir in the shrimp, mushroom soup, salt, chili powder, and ground pepper, then bring to a boil. Mix in the cooked rice and bananas. Spoon into a buttered 1½ quart casserole. Cover. Bake at 375° for 30 minutes or until the mixture is bubbly.

Serves 4 to 6.

Creamed Sea Food

½ cup butter
⅓ cup flour
1 teaspoon salt
2 cups milk
½ cup chopped onion
2 teaspoons lemon juice
1 (7 ounce) can Alaska snow
   crab & liquid

1 (8 ounce) package frozen
   Alaska shrimp, cooked &
   peeled
½ cup chopped parsley
Tabasco sauce
2 egg yolks
Steamed rice

Melt the butter in a saucepan over low heat. Blend in the flour, salt, and add the milk. Bring to a boil and boil 1 minute, stirring constantly. Add the chopped onion, lemon juice, crab and liquid from the crab, and shrimp; simmer gently for about 5 minutes or until the shrimp are thawed. Add parsley and a few drops of Tabasco sauce. Mix together well. Beat the egg yolks, add a little hot sauce while stirring, and then add to the sauce. Simmer, stirring constantly, until the egg yolks are cooked. Check for seasoning. Serve over steamed rice if desired.

Serves 6.

Shrimp Scampi

2 pounds shrimp, shelled
  & deveined
⅓ cup olive oil
½ cup extra dry vermouth
2 cloves garlic, crushed

¾ teaspoon salt
½ teaspoon ground black
   pepper
3 tablespoons chopped
   parsley
3 tablespoons lemon juice

Brown the shrimp in hot olive oil. Add the vermouth, garlic, salt, and pepper. Cook until the liquid is almost gone. Sprinkle with parsley and lemon juice and serve.

Serves 4.

Poultry

Chicken

Oven Crisp Chicken

1 (2½-3 pound) frying
    chicken, cut up
½ cup melted butter
¼ cup white table wine
1 cup corn flake crumbs

¾ teaspoon salt
½ teaspoon onion or
    garlic salt
¼ teaspoon thyme
¼ teaspoon paprika

Rinse the chicken and pat dry. Combine the melted butter and wine in a pie plate or shallow dish. Mix the corn flake crumbs, salt, onion or garlic salt, thyme, and paprika in a paper bag. Shake to mix well. Dip the pieces of chicken in the butter-wine mixture; then shake 2 or 3 pieces at a time with the seasoned crumbs, coating the chicken evenly. Place the chicken, skin side up, in a shallow baking pan lined with aluminum foil. (Do not crowd the pieces.) Sprinkle with any remaining wine-butter mixture. Bake, uncovered, at 350° for 1 hour or until the chicken is tender. No turning is necessary. Serve with creamy scalloped potatoes and a green vegetable.

Variation: The wine-butter mixture may be replaced by ⅔ cup undiluted evaporated milk.

Serves 4.

Cheese-Chicken Enchiladas

2 cans cream of chicken soup
1 cup milk
2 (4 ounce) cans chopped
    jalapeno peppers

1 dozen flour tortillas
1½ pounds Monterey Jack
    cheese, grated
2 cups diced, cooked
    chicken

Stir together the chicken soup, milk, and peppers. Tender fry the tortillas in oil or butter until soft. Dip the tortillas, one at a time, in the soup mixture, then fill with cheese and chicken and roll. Arrange in a greased baking dish with seams down. Cover with the remaining sauce. Top with the remaining cheese. Bake at 425° for 15-20 minutes.

Serves 4 to 6.

Stir-Fry Chicken

2 whole chicken breasts,
   skinned, boned, & cubed
3 tablespoons vegetable oil
½ teaspoon salt
2 green onions
1 (7 ounce) package frozen
   Chinese pea pods or
   1 (10 ounce) package
   frozen peas, thawed
2 tablespoons sliced pimento
   (optional)

1 cup sliced fresh mushrooms
   or 1 (3 ounce) can sliced
   mushrooms, drained
1 tablespoon cornstarch
1 (10 ounce) can chicken
   broth
¼ cup toasted
   slivered almonds
White rice, cooked

In a skillet or wok, stir-fry the chicken in vegetable oil over medium to high heat until tender. Remove from the skillet and sprinkle with salt. Set aside. Into the skillet, add the onions, diagonally sliced, pea pods or thawed peas, pimento, and mushrooms; stir-fry 1 minute. Sprinkle with cornstarch. Stir in the chicken broth and simmer, stirring frequently, until thickened. Add the slivered almonds and chicken and heat through. Serve over hot cooked rice.

Serves 4.

Chicken Livers Gourmet

2 tablespoons butter
1 medium onion,
   finely chopped
2 pounds mushrooms, sliced
   or 2 (8 ounce) cans sliced
   mushrooms, drained

2 pounds chicken livers
1 ½ tablespoons soy sauce
2 ½ tablespoons chili sauce
1 ½ cups sour cream
1 ½ cups dry red wine
Salt
Freshly ground pepper

In a skillet, melt the butter. Sauté the onion in the butter until it begins to brown. Stir in the mushrooms and sauté for 3-4 minutes. Add the chicken livers and sauté quickly until they have lost all their pinkness. Combine the soy sauce, chili sauce, sour cream, and wine. Stir into the chicken livers, and season to taste with salt and freshly ground pepper. Serve hot on biscuits, rice seasoned with chicken broth, or crêpes.

(You can refrigerate for later use.) To serve, bring to room temperature and heat through gently. Do not allow to boil or the sour cream will curdle.

Serves 6.

Oven-Baked Chicken Kiev

7 tablespoons butter
  or margarine, softened
2 tablespoons chopped parsley
½ teaspoon leaf tarragon,
  crumbled
¼ teaspoon salt
⅛ teaspoon pepper

3 whole chicken breasts
  (about 2½ pounds)
1½ cups unseasoned
  bread crumbs
2 tablespoons flour
1 egg

Combine 6 tablespoons butter, parsley, tarragon, salt, and pepper in a small bowl. Spread this mixture on wax paper to a 4x3-inch rectangle. Place the mixture in the refrigerator to chill. Split the chicken breasts; remove skin; carefully cut meat from bones, keeping meat in whole pieces (6 in all). Place each piece, smooth side down, between 2 sheets of wax paper. Flatten with a wooden mallet to about ¼-inch thickness, being careful not to break the meat. Remove the parsley butter from the refrigerator. Cut into 6 equal finger-size pieces. Place a "finger" of the parsley-butter in the center of each flattened chicken breast. Bring the long sides of the chicken over the butter; then fold the ends over, being sure the butter is completely covered. Fasten with wooden picks. Thoroughly combine the bread crumbs and 1 table-spoon butter together on wax paper; place the flour on another piece of wax paper. Beat the egg in a small bowl. Roll each chicken roll completely in the flour, then the egg, then in the crumb mixture to coat completely and evenly. Place the chicken rolls in a single layer in a jelly roll pan. Bake at 425° for 5 minutes. Lower heat to 400° and bake 25 minutes longer. Serve with hot bulgur, if you wish.

This dish may be baked right away or stashed in the freezer for a quick dinner anytime.

Serves 6.

Batter Baked Chicken

1 (3-3½ pound) fryer, cut up
  or equal amount of
  favorite parts
1 egg, beaten
½ cup milk
1 cup flour

1 teaspoon baking powder
2 teaspoons salt
2 teaspoons paprika
¼ teaspoon pepper
¼ cup chopped pecans
2 tablespoons sesame seeds
½ cup butter

Rinse and pat dry the chicken. Combine the egg and milk. Combine the flour, baking powder, salt, paprika, pepper, pecans, and sesame seeds. Dip the chicken into the milk mixture, then into the flour mixture. Melt the butter in a shallow baking pan in a hot oven, 400°. Remove the baking pan from the oven. As pieces of floured chicken are placed in the pan, turn to coat with butter, then bake skin side down in a single layer. Bake at 400° for 30 minutes. Turn the chicken and bake another 30 minutes, or until tender, at 350°. If the chicken cannot be served at once, reduce oven heat and brush chicken with more melted butter.

Serves 4.

Braised Chicken with Zucchini

1 (2½ pound) broiler-fryer
  chicken
¼ teaspoon salt
1 (8 ounce) can whole peeled
  tomatoes, reserve liquid
1 tablespoon olive oil or
  vegetable oil

½ teaspoon minced &
  peeled garlic
1 cube chicken bouillon
1 pound zucchini, washed &
  cut into 1-inch cubes
  (about 3½ cups)
¼ cup chopped fresh parsley

Rinse the chicken and pat dry. Heat the broiler. Sprinkle the chicken with salt. Place, skin side down, on a rack in a broiler pan. Broil 3-4 inches from the heat for 10 minutes. Turn the chicken pieces and broil 5 minutes longer. Place the reserved tomato liquid in a measuring cup and fill to 1 cup with water. In a large skillet, heat the olive oil over moderate heat. Add the minced garlic and cook for 30 seconds. Add the tomatoes and cook 3 minutes, breaking up with a spoon and stirring often. Stir in the reserved tomato liquid mixture and bouillon cube, and bring to a boil. Place the chicken in a single layer in a skillet. Baste with the sauce and simmer 20 minutes, turning the chicken and basting once. Add the zucchini and parsley. Recover and cook 5 minutes longer, until the zucchini is crisp-tender.

This dish has only 303 calories per serving.

Serves 4.

Oven Barbecue Chicken

2 broiler-fryer chickens
1 teaspoon hickory-
   smoked salt
¼ teaspoon pepper
1 large onion, sliced &
   separated into rings
½ cup water

Katherine's Favorite
   Barbecue Sauce:
1 cup catsup
1 cup wine vinegar
¾ cup brown sugar
¾ cup chili sauce
3 tablespoons steak sauce
2 tablespoons
   Worcestershire sauce
2 tablespoons prepared
   mustard
½ teaspoon pepper
2 cloves garlic, minced

Place the legs, thighs, and breasts of the chickens skin side up in a 13x9x2-inch pan. Sprinkle lightly with the hickory-smoked salt and pepper. Top with the onion rings. Pour the water around the chicken. Bake, uncovered, at 375° for 30 minutes. Pour your favorite barbecue sauce over the chicken or use **Katherine's Favorite Barbecue Sauce.** Continue baking the chicken for 30 minutes.

Katherine's Favorite Barbecue Sauce: Combine all ingredients in a saucepan. Bring to a boil. Reduce heat and simmer for 15 minutes.

Serves 6, with 3½ cups sauce.

87

Washington Chicken with California Sunshine

½ cup flour
½ teaspoon paprika
1 teaspoon salt
1 ½ teaspoons seasoned salt
1 (2½-3 pound) fryer, cut up
¼ cup oil
¼ cup butter
3 shallots, peeled & sliced

¾ cup Sauterne
¼ cup orange juice
1 tablespoon lemon juice
1 ½ teaspoons grated orange
  peel
1 ½ teaspoons grated lemon
  peel
¼ cup finely chopped parsley

Mix together the flour, paprika, salt, and seasoned salt. Coat the cut up fryer with the flour mixture. Add the oil and butter to a skillet and heat until the butter is melted; hold at medium heat (350°). Add the shallots and the chicken, and cook until golden brown. Place in a 3 quart casserole. Pour off any fat remaining in the pan. Add the Sauterne, orange juice, lemon juice, orange peel, lemon peel, and parsley. Heat to simmering. Pour over the chicken. Cover and bake at 325° for 1 hour. (If you wish to cook on top of the range in a skillet, cover and cook gently until tender.) Serve with mashed potatoes, vegetable, and baked apple.

Serves 4.

Chicken Waikiki Beach

2 whole chicken legs
2 whole chicken breasts
½ cup flour
⅓ cup salad oil or shortening
1 teaspoon salt
¼ teaspoon pepper
1 (20 ounce) can sliced
   pineapple

1 cup sugar
2 tablespoons cornstarch
¾ cup cider vinegar
1 tablespoon soy sauce
¼ teaspoon ginger
1 cube chicken bouillon
1 large green pepper,cut
   crosswise in ¼-inch rings
White rice, cooked

Wash the chicken legs; separate legs and thighs. Cut the chicken breasts in halves and rinse. Pat dry with paper towels. Coat the chicken with flour. Heat the salad oil or shortening in a large skillet. Add the chicken, a few pieces at a time, and brown on all sides. Remove when browned to shallow roasting pan, arranging pieces skin side up. Sprinkle with salt and pepper. Drain a can of sliced pineapple, pouring the syrup into a 2 cup measure. Add enough water to make 1¼ cups. In a medium saucepan, combine the sugar, cornstarch, pineapple juice, vinegar, soy sauce, ginger, and bouillon cube. Bake, uncovered, at 350° for 30 minutes. Add the pineapple slices and green pepper. Bake 30 minutes longer or until the chicken is tender. Serve with fluffy white rice.

Serves 4.

Chicken Asparagus Casserole

3 cups diced, cooked
  chicken
1 (14½ ounce) can
  asparagus, drained
1½ cups bread cut into
  ½-inch cubes
½ cup slivered almonds
3 eggs, slightly beaten
1 cup chicken broth
1½ teaspoons lemon juice

½ teaspoon salt
1 teaspoon onion juice

Mushroom Sauce:
½ pound mushrooms, sliced
3 tablespoons butter
2 tablespoons flour
1 cup chicken broth
½ cup heavy cream
½ teaspoon salt

Layer the chicken, asparagus, and bread cubes in a buttered 2 quart casserole. Top with the almonds. Combine the eggs, broth, lemon juice, salt, and onion juice. Pour over the ingredients in the casserole. Bake at 350° for 1 hour. Serve with **Mushroom Sauce.**

Mushroom Sauce: Sauté the mushrooms in butter. Add the flour and stir to combine. Add the chicken broth and cook until thickened. Stir in the cream and salt.

Serves 6 to 8.

Puget Sound Chicken

½ cup flour
1½ teaspoons salt
¼ teaspoon pepper
5 slices bacon
2 fryers: breast halves,
    thighs, legs

1 cup Burgundy wine
¼ cup water
1 (4 ounce) can mushroom
    stems & pieces,
    with liquid
1 (1 pound) can cherry pie
    filling

Combine the flour, 1 teaspoon salt, and pepper in a paper bag. Add the chicken pieces, a few at a time, and shake until coated with flour. Remove from the bag and set aside. In a skillet, fry the bacon until crisp. Remove it from the pan, crumble, and set aside. In the bacon drippings, fry the chicken until golden brown. Place the chicken in a 2½-3 quart casserole. Sprinkle with ½ teaspoon salt. Pour off the excess fat from the skillet. Add the wine, water, mushrooms, and cherry pie filling to the skillet. Add the crumbled bacon. Heat to simmering. Pour the sauce over the chicken in the casserole. Bake at 350° for 1 hour. If Pyrex is used, lower the temperature to 325°.

Serves 6.

Dinner Party Chicken

4 whole chicken breasts or
    8 large chicken breasts,
    halved & boned
Flour
6 tablespoons butter
1½ cups sliced celery
1 medium onion, minced
6 tablespoons flour
1 teaspoon salt

¼ teaspoon pepper
3 cups milk
1 (10¾ ounce) can
    mushroom soup, undiluted
2 cups cubed cooked ham
2 tablespoons minced pimento
¼ teaspoon dried basil
3 tablespoons sherry
½ cup grated sharp
    cheddar cheese

Dip the chicken breasts in flour. Brown the chicken in butter in a large skillet. Set aside the chicken. Sauté the celery and onion in the butter and drippings in the skillet. Cook until tender. Stir in the flour, salt,

90

pepper, and then add the milk. Cook until the sauce thickens, stirring constantly. Add the mushroom soup, cooked ham, minced pimento, dried basil, and sherry. Combine all and then pour half the sauce in a buttered 3 quart casserole or large, shallow baking dish. Place the browned chicken over the sauce. Add the remaining sauce and top with the grated sharp cheddar cheese. Bake at 350° for 1 hour.

Serves 6 to 8.

Chicken Tahitian

6 chicken breasts, boned & halved	6 tablespoons flour
2 tablespoons lemon juice	2 cups milk
1 ½ teaspoons ground ginger	1 cup unsweetened pineapple juice
6 tablespoons butter	4 cups cooked rice
1 teaspoon salt	½ cup chopped macadamia nuts
¼ teaspoon pepper	

Marinate the chicken in the lemon juice seasoned with 1 teaspoon ground ginger. Broil the breasts for 10 minutes on each side, dotting them with butter. Sprinkle with salt and pepper. Stir together over low heat 6 tablespoons pan drippings and the flour. Remove from heat and stir in the milk. Return to heat and cook until very thick. Add the pineapple juice and ½ teaspoon ground ginger. In the bottom of a casserole, place the chicken breasts and rice. Cover all with the sauce to which you add macadamia nuts. Bake, uncovered, at 350° for 20-30 minutes.

Serves 6.

Roast Quarters of Chicken

1 whole frying chicken
½ cup dry white table wine
¼ cup butter
3 tablespoons olive oil
1 onion, finely chopped

1 tablespoon chopped parsley
⅛ teaspoon garlic powder
   (optional)
½ teaspoon salt
1 teaspoon crushed oregano
1 (4 ounce) can mushrooms

Rinse the chicken and pat dry. Cut the chicken in half and then in quarters or use 2 broiler halves. Place the chicken in a baking dish and add the wine. Allow to marinate at least 1 hour, turning occasionally. Drain the marinade into a saucepan. Place the chicken in a baking dish; broil golden brown on both sides. Heat the marinade with the butter, olive oil, onion, parsley, garlic powder, salt, and oregano. Bring to a boil and pour over the chicken. Bake at 350° for 45 minutes, basting occasionally. Add the mushrooms and the liquid. Heat through and serve.

Serves 4.

Barbecued Chicken

2 tablespoons cornstarch
2 (8 ounce) cans
   tomato sauce
¾ cup corn oil
½ cup soy sauce

⅓ cup lime juice
2 tablespoons sugar
1 tablespoon garlic powder
2 teaspoons ground ginger
2 broiler-fryer chickens,
   cut up

Blend the cornstarch in a saucepan with part of the tomato sauce, gradually stirring in the remaining tomato sauce. Add the corn oil, soy sauce, lime juice, sugar, garlic powder, and ginger. Cook, stirring constantly, until the mixture boils. Boil about 2 minutes. Cool. Place the chickens in a large bowl and pour the sauce over the chicken. Cover and refrigerate 2 hours or longer. Place the chicken in a single layer, skin side up, on a rack in a large, shallow baking pan. Bake at 350°, uncovered, for 1 hour or until fork tender. Baste several times during the baking with the sauce used as a marinade.

Serves 6 to 8.

Pheasant

Pheasant

1 pheasant
¾ cup butter
1 large onion, chopped
2 stalks celery, chopped
1 cup chopped mushrooms,
  fresh or canned

1 teaspoon salt
1 teaspoon pepper
¼ teaspoon poultry seasoning
1½ cups Burgundy wine
Brown rice

Joint the pheasant and brown in butter. Remove from the pan and add the onion, celery, mushrooms, and spices. Sauté the mushroom mixture, gradually stirring in the Burgundy. Simmer slowly about 15 minutes. Return the pheasant to the pan and allow to simmer gently until done (about 50-60 minutes for a young bird and 1½-2 hours for an older bird). Serve with brown rice covered with wine-mushroom sauce.

Serves 4.

Roast Pheasant

1 plump young pheasant
  (2-3 pounds dressed)
Salt & pepper
1 bay leaf
1 clove garlic, crushed
Celery leaves
1 slice lemon

4 slices bacon
Melted butter
1 large onion, sliced
2 (4 ounce) cans button
  mushrooms
1 cup chicken broth
Rice

Sprinkle the pheasant inside and out with salt and pepper. Place the bay leaf, garlic, a few celery leaves, and a slice of lemon in the cavity. Tie the legs together with string. Turn the wings under. Cover the breast with the bacon and a cheesecloth soaked in melted butter. Place the pheasant, breast side up, in a baking pan. Arrange the onion slices and mushrooms with liquid around the pheasant. Pour the chicken broth (canned or made with 1 cube chicken bouillon dissolved in 1 cup hot water) over the pheasant. Roast at 350° for 30 minutes per pound or until tender, basting frequently with the liquid in the pan. Remove the cheesecloth and string. Serve with rice.

This recipe is also excellent with chicken substituted for pheasant.

Serves 3 to 4.

Turkey

Keith Jackson's Up-to-Date Turkey Stuffing

1 cup finely chopped onion
1 cup finely chopped celery
½ cup chopped parsley
1 cup butter or margarine
*1 (8 ounce) package herb-
  seasoned stuffing*
*1 (8 ounce) package corn
  bread stuffing*

½ cup wheat germ
2 teaspoons rubbed sage
2 teaspoons salt
½ teaspoon pepper
2 eggs, slightly beaten
*2-2½ cups broth from giblets
  or water*

Sauté the onion, celery, and parsley in butter or margarine. Place the stuffing mix in a large bowl. Add the sautéed onion mixture and toss lightly. Add the wheat germ, seasonings, slightly beaten eggs, and 2 cups broth. Mix thoroughly. The stuffing should be moist enough to hold its shape when pressed. Add more broth if needed. Pack the stuffing lightly into the body of the turkey. Fasten with skewers and lace with string. Stuff the neck cavity and fasten with skewers. Brush with melted butter. Place the turkey on a trivet in an uncovered roasting pan, without water. Follow roasting time and temperature given on the turkey wrapper or use the directions given below.

Makes enough stuffing for 12-14 pound bird.

Roasting Turkey: Roast the turkey at 325° on a rack in a shallow open pan.

Weight	Stuffed
4-8 pounds	3-3½ hours
8-12 pounds	3½-4 hours
12-16 pounds	4-4½ hours
16-20 pounds	4½-5 hours
20-24 pounds	5-6 hours

Roasting times are approximate as variations in ovens, shape of turkey, and degree of thawing will affect the time. Turkey is done when meat thermometer registers 180°-185°. When degree of browning is reached, a "tent" of lightweight foil, shiny side down, may be placed loosely over the turkey to prevent over-browning.

Roast Turkey with Onion Sage Stuffing

1 (6-8 pound) turkey,
 ready-to-roast
Salt
2 cups chicken broth

Onion Sage Stuffing:
1 cup chopped onion
¼ cup finely diced celery

1½ teaspoons sage
½ cup chicken bouillon
2 slices enriched white bread
 cut into ½-inch cubes
8 teaspoons margarine,
 (diet or imitation)
2 teaspoons chopped
 fresh parsley
Dash salt

Place the turkey, breast side up, on a rack in a shallow pan. Season and roast at 325° for 2-2½ hours. Baste every 20 minutes with bouillon until done. Carve portions and serve with stuffing.

Onion Sage Stuffing: Lightly brown the onions, celery, and sage in a nonstick skillet. Remove; add the bouillon and remaining ingredients. Transfer to a casserole and bake 30 minutes (in same oven as turkey). Divide into 4 equal portions and serve with turkey.

Turkey will serve 8, stuffing 4.

Turkey Loaf

1½ pounds ground turkey or
 4 cups ground leftover turkey
½ cup chicken broth
 (more if turkey is dry)
½ cup light cream
2 eggs

1 cup herb seasoned
 stuffing crumbs
1 medium onion, minced
Pinch thyme
Salt & pepper to taste
1 can mushroom soup
½ soup can of milk

Blend the ground turkey with the chicken broth, cream, eggs, crumbs, onion, thyme, salt, and pepper. Place in a greased pan. Bake at 350° for 1 hour or until set. Serve with sauce made from mushroom soup and milk.

Serves 4 to 6.

Cheese & Turkey Bake

1 cup shredded cheddar
  cheese
1 tablespoon flour
1 cup blanched slivered
  almonds
3 cups chopped cooked
  turkey
1 ½ cups celery slices

1 tablespoon lemon juice
1 cup mayonnaise
½ teaspoon poultry seasoning
½ teaspoon salt
⅛ teaspoon pepper
Pastry for 2 crust pie
Lemon twists
Parsley

Toss the cheese with the flour. Combine ¾ cup floured cheese (reserve ¼ cup) with ½ cup almonds, turkey, celery slices, lemon juice, mayonnaise, poultry seasoning, salt, and pepper. Mix well. Roll the pastry into a 15-inch square. Fit the pastry into a 11¾x7½-inch baking dish, trim to 1 inch beyond the edge, and flute the edge. Fill with the turkey mixture. Top with the remaining ¼ cup cheese and ½ cup almonds. Bake at 400° for 30-35 minutes. Garnish with lemon twists and parsley, if desired. To make lemon twists: cut a slice of lemon through the rind to the center and twist into a figure-eight.

Serves 6 to 8.

Swiss Cheese and Turkey Casserole

1 (10 ounce) package frozen
  chopped broccoli
2 (11 ounce) cans cheddar
  cheese soup
¼ teaspoon pepper
¼ teaspoon nutmeg
1 ½ cups grated Swiss cheese

2 teaspoons lemon juice
2 cups cooked turkey,
  cut into strips
1 (2½ ounce) jar sliced
  mushrooms, drained
¼ cup grated Parmesan
  cheese
10 canned refrigerated biscuits

Cook the broccoli according to package directions, drain thoroughly, and set aside. Turn the cheddar soup into a saucepan. Add the pepper, nutmeg, and Swiss cheese. Cook, stirring until the cheese melts. Add the lemon juice, turkey, mushrooms, and broccoli. Pour into a lightly greased 11¾x7½-inch baking dish and sprinkle with Parmesan cheese. Top with the biscuits. Bake at 375° for 20-25 minutes or until biscuits are golden brown.

Serves 6.

Viennese Turkey Pie

3 tablespoons butter
1 cup coarsely chopped onion
2 tablespoons flour
3 eggs, slightly beaten
1 cup dairy sour cream
2 tablespoons dry or medium
   sherry or dry vermouth

1 teaspoon Worcestershire
   sauce
¼ teaspoon paprika
Salt and pepper to taste
1 cup diced, cooked turkey
1 cup shredded cheddar
   cheese
1 tablespoon parsley flakes
1 (9-inch) baked pastry shell

Melt the butter in a saucepan or skillet; add the chopped onion and sauté gently until the onion is tender but not brown. Remove from the heat and stir in the flour. Beat the eggs slightly, and add the sour cream and sherry or vermouth; beat until blended. Add the onion mixture and stir well. Season with Worcestershire sauce, paprika, salt, and pepper. Lightly mix in the turkey, cheddar cheese, and parsley flakes; spread evenly over the bottom of a 9-inch baked pastry shell with high fluted rim. Bake at 350° for about 45 minutes and let stand 10-15 minutes before cutting.

You may use chicken, crabmeat, shrimp, or tuna instead of turkey.

Serves 4 to 6.

Turkey-Chicken Almond Casserole

1 (12 ounce) package
   frozen broccoli
2 tablepoons butter or
   margarine
2 tablespoons flour
1 teaspoon salt
¼ teaspoon dry mustard
¼ teaspoon black pepper

2 cups milk
1 cup grated American cheese
2 cups cooked noodles
2 cups diced cooked
   turkey or chicken
⅓ cup roasted almonds,
   slivered or diced

Cook the broccoli according to package directions. Dice the stems and leave the florets whole. Melt the butter and blend in the flour, salt, mustard, and pepper. Add the milk; cook and stir until the mixture thickens. Remove from heat and stir in the cheese. Pour over the drained noodles. Add the turkey and broccoli stems and mix lightly. Turn into a shallow 8-inch round baking dish. Arrange the broccoli florets on top, pressing lightly into the noodles. Sprinkle with the almond slivers. Bake at 350° for about 15 minutes.

Serves 4 to 6.

Turkey with Curried Pineapple Glaze

1 whole or half turkey breast
Salt
2 teaspoons cornstarch
1 teaspoon curry powder
¼ teaspoon instant minced onion
⅛ teaspoon garlic salt

2 tablespoons cold water
1 (8 ounce) can crushed pineapple
2 tablespoons brown sugar
1 tablespoon butter or margarine
White pepper

Rinse the turkey and pat dry. Sprinkle with salt if desired. Place on a rack in an open roasting pan and roast at 325° for 1½-2 hours for a half breast or 2-2½ hours for a whole breast, or until a meat thermometer inserted in thickest part of breast registers 180°-185°. To make the glaze: mix the cornstarch, curry powder, onion, and garlic salt together, then stir in the cold water. Heat the pineapple with the brown sugar in a small saucepan. Add the cornstarch mixture; stir over low heat until smooth and clear. Add the butter, salt, and white pepper to taste. Spread over the roast turkey breast and return the turkey to the oven for 10 minutes.

Glaze makes about 1 cup.

Chicken or Turkey Pie with Biscuit Topping

2 tablespoons butter
2 tablespoons chopped onion
½ cup celery, chopped
¼ cup chopped green pepper
2 tablespoons flour
¼ teaspoon pepper
1 teaspoon garlic salt
1 cube chicken bouillon
¾ cup milk
1 cup evaporated milk
1½ teaspoons soy sauce
2 cups cooked & chopped
   turkey or chicken

6 slices bacon,
   cooked & crumbled

Biscuit Topping:
2 cups prepared biscuit mix
⅓ cup water
⅓ cup evaporated milk
1 cup shredded sharp
   cheddar cheese
½ cup chopped stuffed olives
Melted butter

Melt the butter in a skillet; add the onion, celery, and green pepper. Sauté until tender. Blend in the flour and seasonings. Dissolve the bouillon cube in the milk, and add to the skillet with the evaporated milk. Add the soy sauce, chicken or turkey, and bacon. Pour into a buttered 1½ quart casserole.

Biscuit Topping: Mix the biscuit mix, water, and evaporated milk together lightly. Roll out to an 8x12-inch rectangle. Combine the cheddar cheese and olives. Spread over the dough and roll up as a jelly roll. Form the roll into a ring and place in the middle of the casserole. Snip partly through with scissors every 1½ inches. (If you prefer, slice and place around on top of the casserole.) Brush the top with melted butter. Bake at 425° for 15-20 minutes or until the casserole has heated through and the topping is brown and done.

Serves 6.

Meat

Beef

Old Time Milwaukee Lasagne

1 pound ground beef
1 clove garlic, minced
2 tablespoons salad oil
1 (20 ounce) can solid
    pack tomatoes
1 (8 ounce) can tomato sauce
1 teaspoon salt
½ teaspoon pepper

½ teaspoon oregano
½ pound lasagne noodles
1 pound ricotta or dry
    cottage cheese
½ cup grated Parmesan
    cheese
½ pound mozzarella cheese,
    sliced

Brown the beef and garlic in oil, stirring with a fork. Add the tomatoes, first draining off half the juice; add the tomato sauce and seasonings. Simmer for 30 minutes. Cook the noodles until just tender, drain, and rinse. Cover the bottom of a large, greased baking dish with 1½ cups of beef mixture. Cover the beef mixture with a layer of noodles. Spread half the ricotta cheese on the noodles, sprinkle with half the Parmesan cheese, and place over this one-third of the mozzarella. Repeat. Top with remaining beef mixture and mozzarella. Bake at 350° for 45 minutes. Let stand 15 minutes after removing from oven. Cut into squares.

Short Ribs in Beer

4 pounds beef short ribs
2 large onions, sliced
1 clove garlic, chopped
2 teaspoons salt
1 teaspoon marjoram

¼ teaspoon pepper
1 teaspoon sugar
1 tablespoon vinegar
¼ cup chopped parsley
1 (12 ounce) can beer

Heat a large, heavy Dutch oven. Brown the ribs in the pan, a few at a time, over medium heat. Start with fat side down and turn occasionally to brown all sides. When ribs are browned, pour off all but 2 tablespoons of fat in the pan. Reduce heat and add onions and garlic. Cook until the onions start to color. Return the ribs to the Dutch oven and add salt, marjoram, pepper, sugar, vinegar, parsley, and beer. Cover and simmer over low heat, stirring occasionally, about 1½ hours, until meat is tender. Correct seasoning if necessary.

Serves 6.

107

Stuffed Hamburgers with Mushroom Sauce

½ cup chopped onion
½ cup chopped green pepper
½ cup chopped celery
2 tablespoons butter
1 cup herbed stuffing mix
1 ½ pounds ground beef

½ cup evaporated milk
1 cup mushroom soup,
   undiluted
1 tablespoon Worcestershire
   sauce
2 tablespoons catsup

Sauté the onion, pepper, and celery in butter or margarine. Prepare the stuffing mix as directed on the package. Add the onion, pepper, and celery. Combine the ground beef and evaporated milk. Divide into 4 patties. Pat each into a 6-inch circle and divide the stuffing into 4 balls. Wrap the meat around the stuffing and seal. Place in a casserole. Combine the mushroom soup, Worcestershire sauce, and catsup. Pour over the meat. Bake at 350° for 45 minutes.

Serves 4.

Steak Teriyaki

1 cup soy sauce
¼ cup honey
¾ cup vegetable oil
2 teaspoons ground ginger
⅓ cup white raisins,
   soaked & drained
1 (8½ ounce) can water
   chestnuts, sliced

½ green pepper, diced
1 (11 ounce) can Mandarin
   oranges, drained
⅓ cup chopped onion
1 (8¼ ounce) can crushed
   pineapple
2 tablespoons vinegar
1 large clove garlic, minced
1 ½ pound flank steak

Combine all ingredients except steak for the marinade. Marinate the meat overnight, if possible, without refrigeration, or at least 6 hours. Drain the meat and place on a barbecue rack or on the broiler near the source of heat. The flank steak is a thin cut and will take approximately 6 minutes on each side for a pink center, or cook it to your desired degree of doneness. Reserve the marinade, draining off the oil from the top as much as possible. Pour into a saucepan and heat over low heat. Serve as a sauce for the meat or over rice.

Serves 4.

Mother's Ground Beef Casserole

1 pound American cheese
1 large onion or 2 large
   green peppers
1 cup carrots

1½ pounds lean ground beef
1 cup raw rice
1 quart milk (excellent
   made with powdered milk)
Salt

Put the cheese, onion or pepper, and carrot through the food chopper or food processor. Combine the remaining ingredients and bake 1½ hours at 350° Serve with mushroom sauce.

Serves 8 to 10.

Beef Jerky

1 flank steak (1½ pounds,
   approximately)
1 teaspoon seasoned salt
⅓ teaspoon garlic powder

⅓ teaspoon black pepper
1 teaspoon onion powder
¼ cup Worcestershire sauce
¼ cup soy sauce

Trim off all possible fat and semi-freeze the meat. Slice it with the grain (the long way) into ⅛-¼-inch slices. Combine the seasonings. Combine the sauce ingredients. Stir a little of the sauce into the seasonings, then combine all together. Cover the bottom of a 9x15x2-inch Pyrex dish with the sauce. Place one layer of flank strips in the sauce. Brush on more sauce. Cover with more strips of meat. Brush on the remaining sauce and marinate overnight. The next day, lay strips of marinated meat in a single layer on the oven racks (place foil underneath to catch drips). Dry at 140° for 6-8 hours, until it is as chewy as desired, tasting occasionally.

Variations: If you wish, add a few drops Liquid Smoke or sherry to the sauce.

Makes approximately ½ pound.

Mock Beef Stroganoff

3 pounds lean ground beef
3 tablespoons butter or
    margarine
1½ teaspoons salt
¼ teaspoon pepper

1½ cups tomato sauce
12 ounces narrow noodles
2 cups dairy sour cream
1 (8 ounce) package cream
    cheese, softened
1 cup grated cheddar cheese

Brown the ground beef in butter or margarine. Stir and mix until crumbled and color has changed. Add the salt, pepper, and tomato sauce. Cook the noodles according to package directions. Drain. Add to the meat mixture. Combine the sour cream with the cream cheese. Add to the meat-noodle mixture and combine all well. Pour the meat mixture into a 2½ quart buttered casserole. Top with the grated cheddar cheese. Bake at 325° for 1 hour.

Serves 8 to 12.

Busy Day Beef Stroganoff

½ cup milk
1 envelope sour cream
    sauce mix
1 pound boneless
    sirloin steak
2 tablespoons butter
1 onion, thinly sliced

1 (4 ounce) can sliced
    mushrooms
¾ cup water
1 envelope brown gravy mix
¼ teaspoon paprika
Rice or noodles
Parsley

Gradually stir the milk into the sour cream sauce mix. Let the mixture stand. Cut the sirloin steak into thin strips (flour meat if desired). Cook the beef in hot butter until the meat is browned. Add the onion and cook until tender. Add the mushrooms and liquid, the water, brown gravy mix, and paprika. Simmer, stirring occasionally. Stir in the sour cream mix and heat, but do not boil. Serve over rice or noodles. Garnish with parsley.

Serves 4.

Berniece's Baloney-Salami

5 heaping teaspoons Morton's
   Tender Quick Salt
5 pounds ground beef
1 tablespoon whole
   mustard seed
1 tablespoon coarse ground
   pepper

1 teaspoon hickory-
   smoked salt
2½ teaspoons garlic salt
½-1 teaspoon garlic powder,
   to taste
1 teaspoon Liquid Smoke

Mix all ingredients by hand in a big bowl, then refrigerate overnight. The next day, mix well and refrigerate again. The following day make 5 equal size rolls the width of the broiler pan. Put the broiler pan on the bottom rack of the oven. Bake for 8 hours at 140°. Turn every 2 hours during the baking. The flavor improves with age. Store in the refrigerator for up to 2 weeks; freeze for longer storage.

Makes 5 rolls.

Beef, Onion & Spinach Supreme

3 medium unpeeled onions
1½ pounds ground beef
1 clove chopped garlic
1 (10 ounce) package frozen
   chopped spinach
1 teaspoon salt
1 teaspoon rosemary,
   crumbled
¼ teaspoon pepper

1 teaspoon (or cube)
   chicken bouillon
1¼ cups water
1 cup light cream
1 cup soft bread crumbs
   (2 slices)
2 tablespoons melted butter
½ cup grated cheddar
   cheese, optional

Boil the onions for 15 minutes. Cool, peel, and cut in half. Brown the ground beef in a skillet. Remove the beef. Sauté the garlic in the same pan. Add the frozen chopped spinach; break it up as it cooks and the liquid evaporates. Return the beef to the pan with the salt, rosemary, pepper, chicken bouillon, and water. Arrange half of the onion in a 13x9x2-inch baking dish. Spoon the meat mixture over the onion. Top with the remaining onion. Pour the cream overall. Cover and bake at 375° for 45 minutes. Combine the bread crumbs with the melted butter and grated cheese. Sprinkle on top of the casserole and bake, uncovered, 10-15 minutes until the bread crumbs are browned.

Beef in Burgundy—the Quick Way

1½ pounds round steak,
  cubed
2 tablespoons butter
1 (10¾ ounce) can beef &
  mushroom soup, undiluted
1 cup Burgundy wine

1 (8 ounce) can mushrooms,
  pieces & stems
1 (16 ounce) can small
  onions, drained
Parsley, minced
Noodles, cooked & hot

Brown the steak in butter in a Dutch oven. Add the soup, Burgundy wine, and liquid from mushrooms. Simmer, uncovered, until tender, about 1½ hours. Add the mushrooms and onions. When hot, sprinkle with parsley and serve with noodles.

Serves 4 to 6.

Ellensburg Beef

2 pounds round steak,
  cut ½-inch thick
½ cup flour
1 teaspoon salt
3 tablespoons butter or
  bacon drippings
1 (1 pound) can
  stewed tomatoes
½ cup dry sherry

½ cup canned consommé
  or bouillon broth
3 large carrots, thinly sliced
1 cup sliced celery
1 medium-size onion, diced
1 large clove garlic, minced
1 bay leaf, crumbled
¼ teaspoon pepper

Trim the excess fat off the steak. Pound the flour mixed with salt into both sides of the meat with a meat tenderizer or the edge of a heavy saucer. Cut the meat across the grain into narrow strips about 2 inches long. Heat the butter in a large, heavy skillet or Dutch oven. Add the meat, a small amount at a time, and brown nicely on all sides. Complete the browning of all meat. Add the tomatoes, sherry, consommé, carrots, celery, onion, garlic, bay leaf, and pepper. Bring to a simmer, then cover and simmer very gently for 1½ hours, or until the meat is fork tender. Stir occasionally. and add a little consommé or water if the gravy becomes too thick. Before serving, taste and add a little salt and pepper if necessary.

Serves 4 to 6.

Round Steak Goulash

1 pound steak
2 tablespoons oil
½ teaspoon salt
¼ teaspoon pepper
1 tablespoon brown sugar
1 large onion, sliced
1 bay leaf

2 cups boiling water
¼ cup water
1 tablespoon vinegar
1 tablespoon paprika
2 tablespoons flour
Snipped parsley
Noodles, cooked

Cut the round steak into ½-inch pieces. Brown the meat in the oil. Add the seasonings, sugar, sliced onion, bay leaf, and boiling water. Cover and simmer 1½ hours. Shake together the remaining water, vinegar, paprika, and flour. Thicken the gravy and simmer 15 minutes longer. Adjust seasonings. Garnish with snipped parsley. Serve with noodles.

Serves 4.

Spaghetti Beef Bake

8 ounces spaghetti,
  cooked
1½ pints dairy sour cream
1 cup thinly sliced
  green onions
1 teaspoon salt

1 pound ground beef
1 (8 ounce) can tomato sauce
½ teaspoon garlic salt
⅛ teaspoon pepper
1 cup shredded cheddar
  cheese

Mix the cooked spaghetti with the sour cream, onions, and ½ teaspoon of the salt. Brown the beef in a skillet over medium heat, stirring frequently. Drain off the excess fat. Stir in the tomato sauce, garlic salt, pepper, and remaining ½ teaspoon salt. Simmer, uncovered, for 5 minutes. In a 2 quart casserole, layer the spaghetti and meat mixtures, beginning with spaghetti and ending with meat. Sprinkle with the cheese. Bake at 350° for 25 minutes or until the cheese is lightly browned.

Serves 6.

Meat Whirl

1 ½ pounds ground beef
1 cup soft bread crumbs
1 egg
2 teaspoons prepared
  horseradish

1 (8 ounce) can tomato sauce
1 ½ cups shredded cheddar
  cheese
1 teaspoon dill seed or
  dill weed

Lightly mix the ground beef, bread crumbs, egg, horseradish, and ½ cup tomato sauce. On waxed paper, pat the meat into a 10x14-inch rectangle. Sprinkle with cheese. Roll from the shorter side, as for a jelly roll; press ends to seal. Carefully transfer to a baking pan, seam side down. Bake at 350° for 45 minutes. Pour ½ cup tomato sauce over the meat. Sprinkle with dill seed or dill weed. Bake an additional 15 minutes. Remove to a warm platter.

Serves 6 to 8.

The Captain's Skillet

2 (15½ ounce) cans spaghetti
  with tomato sauce
1 (7 ounce) can pitted
  ripe olives, drained
1 (6 or 7 ounce) can
  mushrooms
1 (#303) can whole-kernel
  corn

1 (15½ ounce) can meatballs
  with sauce or 1 (12 ounce)
  can corned beef, cubed
1 (#2½) can solid-pack
  tomatoes
3 tablespoons minced
  dehydrated onion
1 cup grated cheese

Combine all ingredients except the cheese in a saucepan and heat. Add the cheese; stir until melted. Taste for seasonings. On short boating or sailing trips, substitute fresh ground beef for canned, browning it first, and then adding the rest of the ingredients. This is also excellent for large shore gatherings.

Serves 8 to 10.

Salisbury Steaks with Wine Sauce

1 ¼ pounds lean beef
1 teaspoon salt
¼ teaspoon garlic salt
¼ teaspoon pepper
¼ teaspoon thyme
3 green onions,
  finely chopped
½ green pepper,
  finely chopped
1 tablespoon finely chopped
  parsley
¼ cup water

Wine Sauce:
¼ pound fresh mushrooms,
  sliced
¼ cup butter
Salt & pepper
1 tablespoon flour
¾ cup beef bouillon
¾ cup dry red wine
⅓ cup tomato catsup
1 teaspoon prepared mustard
1 teaspoon Worcestershire
  sauce
2 tablespoons sherry

Combine all the ingredients in the first column thoroughly. Form into 4 oval patties about ½ inch thick. Broil or barbecue to taste. Serve with **Wine Sauce.**

Wine Sauce: Sauté the mushrooms in the butter, season, then stir in the flour. Add the beef bouillon and wine and stir until the mixture comes to a boil. Stir in the remaining ingredients and then simmer for a few minutes. Serve very hot over the broiled Salisbury steaks.

To prepare ahead of time: The **Wine Sauce** can be prepared the day before or in the morning. The Salisbury steaks can be made into patties and refrigerated either the day before or in the morning.

To freeze: The Salisbury steaks can be made into patties and frozen. The best way to defrost them is overnight in the refrigerator, but if that is not possible, defrost at room temperature for no more than 3 hours. The sauce can be frozen. Reheat gently, then serve as in the above recipe.

To bake as a loaf: Double the recipe for both the steaks and the sauce. Shape the meat into a loaf. Place in a 2½-3 quart casserole. Add the sauce and bake, uncovered, at 325° for 1½ hours.

Serves 4.

Reuben Casserole

1¾ cups fresh or canned
  sauerkraut, drained
½ pound corned beef,
  cooked & thinly sliced
½ pound Swiss cheese,
  shredded
3 tablespoons Thousand
  Island dressing

2 medium tomatoes, thinly
  sliced, or 2 cups canned
  tomatoes
½ cup plus 2 tablespoons
  butter
1 cup crumbled, seasoned
  rye wafers
¼ teaspoon caraway seeds

Layer the sauerkraut in the bottom of a 1½ quart buttered casserole. Top with the sliced corned beef, then with the shredded cheese. Daub the Thousand Island dressing on top of the cheese. Add the tomatoes and dot with 2 tablespoons butter. Melt ½ cup butter in a small saucepan. Sauté the crumbled rye wafers; add the caraway seeds. Spread on top of the other ingredients. Bake at 425° for 30 minutes until bubbly.

Serves 4 to 6.

Meat Loaf Soufflé

1½ pounds ground beef
1 egg, beaten
2 teaspoons salt
½ cup dry bread crumbs or
  Rye Crisp crumbs
½ cup milk
½ cup chopped onion

⅛ teaspoon pepper
1 (14 ounce) package sliced
  cheddar cheese
2 tomatoes, sliced
1 cup dairy sour cream
¾ cup Wondra instant flour
3 eggs, separated

Combine the ground beef, egg, 1½ teaspoons salt, crumbs, milk, onion, and pepper. Press into a 9x9-inch baking dish and bake at 350° for 25 minutes. Drain off the fat. Place the sliced cheese and sliced tomatoes on top. Mix the sour cream, instant flour, egg yolks, and ½ teaspoon salt. Beat until thick and smooth. Fold in the egg whites, beaten stiff, and spread over the meat loaf. Bake at 350° for 30-40 minutes or until golden brown. Let stand for 5 minutes before serving.

Serves 8.

Katy's Bones
Oven-Cooked Meat and Chicken Barbecue

8 short ribs or beef bones
4 meaty spareribs or country-
    style, cut in sections
4-8 chicken wings or bony
    pieces of chicken
4 chicken legs and thighs
1 cup catsup
½ cup chili sauce
¼ cup prepare mustard
¾ cup brown sugar
Freshly ground pepper

¾ cup wine vinegar
½ cup fresh lemon juice
¼ cup thick steak sauce
Dash Tabasco sauce
2 tablespoons Worcestershire
    sauce
½ tablespoon soy sauce
1 tablespoon salad oil
¾ cup beer
Liquid Smoke, to taste

Preheat the oven to 350°. Arrange the shortribs and spareribs in a large baking pan. When the oven is hot, place the pan on the center rack and allow fat to dissolve (approximately 30 minutes). Meanwhile, rinse the chicken and dry. In a large pot, combine the catsup and chili sauce, then stir in the mustard, sugar, and pepper. When well mixed, gradually add the vinegar and lemon juice. Place the pot over low heat and stir in the steak sauce, Tabasco sauce, Worcestershire sauce, soy sauce, and oil. When this mixture is gently bubbling, gradually add the beer. The Liquid Smoke should be added a few drops at a time so that you can taste and decide how much more to add. This is a delicious sauce and should be allowed to simmer, uncovered, for at least 45 minutes. Meanwhile, take the baking pan from the oven and drain off the fat. Add the chicken pieces and arrange so that there is no overlapping. Spoon the barbecue sauce over the meats. Return to the oven for 1 hour. *Note:* If the meat is trimmed and lean, it is not necessary to bake it without the sauce as a first step. Place all meats in the pan, cover with sauce, and bake at 350° for 1½ hours. Serve with rice, bulgur, or spaghetti and tossed salad.

Serves 4.

117

Busy Day Stew

1½ pounds ground beef
¾ cup quick or old-fashioned
  oats, uncooked
2 tablespoons parsley flakes
1½ teaspoons salt
¼ teaspoon pepper
⅛ teaspoon garlic powder
¼ cup milk
1 egg
3 tablespoons vegetable oil
2 (10½ ounce) cans
  beef broth, undiluted
1 (8 ounce) can tomato sauce

1 (1 pound) can small
  white potatoes, drained
1 (1 pound) can white
  onions, drained
1 (1 pound) can baby carrots,
  drained
1 (10 ounce) package frozen
  lima beans
¾ teaspoon marjoram
¼ teaspoon powdered thyme
3 cups water
½ cup red wine
½ cup flour

Combine the ground beef, oats, parsley flakes, 1 teaspoon salt, pepper, garlic powder, milk, and egg. Heat the vegetable oil in a Dutch oven. Drop the meat mixture into the fat, one tablespoon at a time. Stir and cook until browned and crumbled. Add the beef broth and tomato sauce. Add the potatoes, onions, carrots, frozen lima beans, marjoram, thyme, ½ teaspoon salt, and 2 cups water. Bring to a boil, then lower heat. Simmer for 20 minutes. Remove the meat and vegetables to a serving dish. Combine 1 cup water, red wine, and flour. Stir until smooth and pour into the beef broth mixture. Bring to a boil, stirring constantly. Cook and stir until thickened. Pour over the meat and vegetable mixture.

Serves 6.

Middle Eastern Meatballs

1 cup bulgur wheat
1 cup cold water
1 pound lean ground beef
1 cup chopped, peeled onion
1 teaspoon salt
½ teaspoon ground allspice

½ teaspoon ground
  black pepper
3 cups beef broth
2 cups plain low-fat yogurt
1 large egg
1 tablespoon cornstarch

Mix the bulgur and water in a large bowl. Let the mixture soak about 20 minutes. Squeeze dry by pressing the bulgur with hands while tipping

118

the bowl to drain off the water. Add the beef, onion, salt, allspice, and ¼ teaspoon pepper to the bulgur. Knead 5-7 minutes to combine thoroughly. Form the mixture into balls, using about 1½ tablespoons for each. Continue with the recipe or refrigerate the meatballs up to 24 hours in a covered, shallow plastic storage container. *To cook:* In a 3-4 quart saucepot, bring the beef broth to a boil over moderately high heat. Add the meatballs, and when boiling, reduce heat and simmer, uncovered, 20 minutes, stirring gently two or three times. In a medium-size bowl, whisk the yogurt, egg, cornstarch, and remaining ¼ teaspoon pepper until smooth. Gently stir into the simmering broth, stir until boiling, then simmer 3 minutes. Remove from heat. Serve soon or cover and refrigerate up to 4 days. These meatballs may be served hot or cold.

Makes 10 cups or 8 to 10 servings.

Chili Cheese Casserole

1 pound ground beef
2 tablespoons butter
1 medium onion, chopped
1 (8 ounce) can tomato sauce
1 (1¾ ounce) package chili
   seasoning mix
½ cup water
2 eggs

1 cup evaporated milk
1 (6 ounce) package
   corn chips
8 ounces Monterey Jack
   cheese, cubed
½ pint sour cream
½ cup cheddar cheese,
   shredded

Brown the ground beef until crumbly. Melt the butter in a skillet. Add the onion and sauté until just tender. Add the tomato sauce, chili seasoning mix, and water. Simmer 5 minutes. Beat the eggs slightly. Add the evaporated milk and mix well. Remove the tomato mixture from the heat and add the egg mixture slowly, stirring constantly. Place half of the corn chips in the bottom of a buttered 2 quart casserole. Top with half the browned meat, then with a layer of half the Monterey Jack cheese. Cover with half the sauce. Repeat the layers. Top with the sour cream and sprinkle the shredded cheddar cheese over. Bake at 325° for 25-30 minutes.

Serves 6 to 8.

Meat and Spinach Soufflé

½ cup chopped onion
2 tablespoons butter
1 pound lean ground beef
1 (10 ounce) package frozen
   chopped spinach
1 cup grated sharp
   cheddar cheese
1 teaspoon salt
¼ teaspoon pepper
6 eggs

1 cup herb seasoned
   stuffing crumbs

Tomato Sauce:
1 medium onion
3 sprigs parsley
1 clove garlic
1 small green pepper
3 tablespoons olive oil
1 (8 ounce) can tomato sauce
Salt & pepper
1 tablespoon butter

Sauté the onion in butter. Add the ground beef. Separate the meat with a fork and cook until the color changes. Add the spinach, cooked and drained. Add the cheese, salt, and pepper. Lightly beat 5 eggs, then mix thoroughly into the meat mixture. Butter a 2½ quart baking dish and sprinkle with ½ cup herb seasoned crumbs. Spread the meat mixture evenly over the crumbs, patting down with a spoon. Beat the remaining egg and spread over the top. Sprinkle with ½ cup seasoned crumbs. Bake at 325° for 30-40 minutes or until set. Serve with **Tomato Sauce.**

Tomato Sauce: Chop the onion, parsley, garlic, and green pepper. Cook in olive oil. Add the tomato sauce. Season with salt and pepper, simmering about 40 minutes while the soufflé is baking. Add the butter before serving.

Serve 6.

Boeuf au Vin

4 pounds beef chuck or round,
   cubed with fat removed
2 tablespoons oil or
   rendered fat from meat
1 large onion, finely diced
¼ cup flour
2 teaspoons salt
¼-½ teaspoon pepper
1 tablespoon chopped parsley
1 bay leaf
¼ teaspoon thyme

¼ teaspoon garlic salt
2 tablespoons tomato puree
Juice of 1 lemon
2 cups sherry, Burgundy
   wine, or broth
1 beef bouillon cube,
   dissolved in
1 cup hot water
2 (4 ounce) cans mushrooms
   & liquid
Spiced apples

In a Dutch oven or heavy skillet, brown the meat in oil a few pieces at a time. Remove from the kettle and set aside. Add the onion to the kettle and cook slightly. Return the meat to the kettle and sprinkle flour, salt, and pepper over the meat; stir. Add the remaining ingredients and bring to a simmering point. Cover and bake at 350° for 2 hours. Serve over patty shells, rice, or noodles. Garnish with spiced apples.

Serves 8.

Jackpot Casserole

1 pound ground beef
2 tablespoons fat
¼ cup chopped onion
1 can condensed tomato soup
1½ cups water
4 ounces noodles

Salt & pepper to taste
1 (#2) can cream-style corn
¼ cup chopped ripe olives
1 cup grated American cheese
2 teaspoons Worcestershire
   sauce

Brown the meat in hot fat, add the onion, and cook until golden. Add the tomato soup, water, and noodles. Cook until the noodles are tender, stirring frequently. Season. Add the corn, olives, ½ cup cheese, and Worcestershire sauce. Pour into a greased 2 quart casserole. Sprinkle with the remaining grated cheese. Bake at 350° for 45 minutes.

Serves 8.

Marinated Beef Roast

1½ cups tomato juice
⅓ cup salad oil
3 tablespoons lime juice
1 tablespoon brown sugar
1 tablespoon Worcestershire
   sauce
2 teaspoons salt

¼ teaspoon hot sauce
3 tablespoons green onion,
   sliced
3½-4½ pounds boneless beef
   rump roast, rolled
1 (14 ounce) can artichoke
   hearts, drained

Combine the tomato juice, oil, lime juice, brown sugar, Worcestershire sauce, salt, and hot sauce. Stir to dissolve the sugar; add the onions. Place the meat and marinade in a plastic bag. Tie the bag securely, place in a pan in the refrigerator, and marinate 6 hours (or overnight), turning occasionally. Remove the roast, reserving marinade, and place on a rack in an open roasting pan. Insert a roast meat thermometer so that the bulb is centered in the thickest part of the roast. Do not add water and do not cover. Roast in a slow oven at 325° to desired degree of doneness: 140° for rare or 160° for medium. Brush with the marinade occasionally during roasting. Allow 2-2½ hours cooking time. Halve the artichokes lengthwise, add to remaining marinade, and cook slowly 5-10 minutes. Remove the artichokes from the marinade and use to garnish the roast. *Note:* A rump roast is best carved in thin slices. For easier carving, allow the roast to stand in a warm place for 15-20 minutes after removal from the oven. Since the roast usually continues to cook after removal from the oven, it is best to remove it at about 5° below the temperature desired.

Serves 6 to 10.

Lamb

Barbecued Butterfly Leg of Lamb

1 (5-6 pound) leg of lamb
Powdered rosemary
Pepper

Sauce:
1 (8 ounce) can tomato sauce

1 teaspoon celery salt
1 teaspoon garlic salt
1 clove garlic, crushed
3 tablespoons olive oil
2 tablespoons red
  wine vinegar
⅓ cup dry sherry

Prepare the lamb by having the butcher bone the leg of lamb: cut so that it will lay out flat in 1 strangely shaped piece. Rub the lamb with powdered rosemary and pepper. Barbecue over coals for about 50 minutes or broil 6-8 inches from moderate heat. Turn and baste about every 15 minutes with the **Sauce.**

Sauce: Simmer together for 15 minutes the tomato sauce, celery salt, garlic salt, garlic, olive oil, and vinegar. Add the sherry after 12 minutes of simmering.

This main course is delicious served with grilled tomatoes, green beans with water chestnuts, toasted French bread, and **Apricot Fluff Pie.**

Serves 8 to 10.

Lamb Stew

2 pounds lamb shoulder
Flour
2 onions, sliced
Salt & pepper
Paprika

2 cups whole pack canned
  tomatoes, drained &
  juice reserved
½ cup chopped celery
1 cup sour cream

Have the lamb shoulder trimmed and cut into 1½-inch cubes. Dredge the meat in flour and brown in hot fat with the sliced onions. Season with salt, pepper, and paprika. Add the whole tomatoes and celery. Simmer slowly about 2 hours, adding the juice from the tomatoes only if necessary during cooking. Just before serving, blend in the sour cream. Heat, but do not boil.

Serves 4.

Stuffed Leg of Lamb

1 (6-7 pound) leg of lamb
1 pound meat loaf mix
  (equal portions of beef,
  veal, & pork)
½ teaspoon marjoram
⅛ teaspoon nutmeg
¼ cup fine dry bread crumbs
¼ cup wheat germ
½ teaspoon garlic flakes
1 egg
1 teaspoon salt

1 (4 ounce) can mushrooms,
  drained, with liquid reserved
Butter
Salt & pepper
1 cup beef bouillon,
  consommé, or broth
¾ cup red table wine
½ teaspoon thyme
¼ teaspoon garlic salt
¼ teaspoon pepper
½ teaspoon savory

Bone the leg of lamb, keeping the cavity as intact as possible for easy stuffing. Mix the meat loaf mix. Add the marjoram, nutmeg, bread crumbs, wheat germ, garlic, egg, and salt. Blend thoroughly, using hands. Chop the mushrooms; add to the meat mixture, blending well. Stuff the meat mixture inside the cavity of the lamb until it is completely filled. Close the cavity by sewing with twine or using skewers. (Flaps of skin should be left on for sewing, but if not, a piece of smoked bacon rind can be used to patch the opening. It also adds flavor.) Rub the roast with butter; season with salt and pepper. Place in a roasting pan and roast at 325° for 35 minutes per pound. Baste every 30 minutes with a mixture of bouillon, wine, thyme, garlic salt, pepper, and savory. Heat the basting mixture in a saucepan and simmer a few minutes. When all of it is used, baste with the pan juices.

Serves 10 to 12.

Lamb Chop Rack

1 ½-2 pound lamb chop rack
  (about 7-8 chops)
½ teaspoon marjoram
½ teaspoon rosemary
½ teaspoon garlic salt

¼ teaspoon pepper
½ cup Italian-style
  bread crumbs
2 tablespoons Dijon mustard
¼ cup butter or margarine,
  melted

Wipe the lamb with damp paper towels; trim off all fat. Place the lamb, using the ribs as a rack, in a shallow, open, roasting pan. Roast uncovered at 375° for 15 minutes per pound of trimmed weight. Remove the roast from the oven; let cool about 15 minutes. Place the spices, salt, and pepper in a bowl and crush. Add the bread crumbs and mix. Spread mustard over the top of the lamb. Pat the crumb mixture into the mustard, pressing firmly. Drizzle with butter. Insert a meat thermometer into the center of the middle chop. Roast 35-40 minutes or until thermometer registers 175° for medium well; roast 5-10 minutes less for medium rare. For rare, the thermometer should read 160°.

Serves 4.

New Zealand Lamb Curry

2 tablespoons butter or fat
2/3 cup onion, chopped
1 1/2 cups apple, cut into
    1/2-inch cubes
2 tablespoons sultana raisins
1 1/2 tablespoons shredded
    coconut
1 teaspoon curry powder
3/4 teaspoon salt

1/4 teaspoon pepper
1 1/3 cups water or
    coconut milk
2 cups cooked lamb, beef or
    fowl, cut into 1-inch cubes
1 large firm banana, sliced
Cooked rice
Assorted condiments

Melt the butter in a pan and fry the onion until it starts to color. Add the apple and stir. Add the raisins and coconut and mix well. Add the curry powder, salt, and pepper. Fry all for 5 minutes, stirring until well blended. Add the water or coconut milk and the cooked meat. Cover the pan tightly, and cook for at least 1 1/2 hours at 250° or on top of the stove on the lowest heat. Uncover and add a little water if the curry has become too dry. It must have the consistency of a thin stew. Add the banana, stir, cover, and cook for another 1/2 hour. Serve with rice and an assortment of condiments, such as salted peanuts, coconut, pineapple chunks, raisins, crumbled bacon, pickled crabapple, tart jelly, chutney, and olives.

Serves 4.

Lamb Chops with Sour Cream

4 lamb shoulder chops
2 tablespoons butter or
   margarine
¼ cup sliced green onions
1 can condensed consommé
¼ teaspoon basil
¼ teaspoon oregano

1 (4 ounce) can sliced
   mushrooms & liquid
3 tablespoons flour
2 tablespoons parsley
½ teaspoon salt
¼ teaspoon pepper
1 cup commercial sour cream
Chopped onion tops
Steamed rice

Brown the lamb in butter or margarine on both sides. Add the green onions and cook until clear. Add the consommé, basil, and oregano. Simmer 30 minutes or until tender. Blend the liquid from the sliced mushrooms with the flour, gradually stir into the mixture, and cook until thick, stirring constantly. Add the mushrooms, parsley, salt, and pepper. Place the sour cream over the chops, cover, and heat for about 2 minutes. Do not boil. Sprinkle with chopped onion tops. Serve over steamed rice.

Serves 4.

Grand Mixed Grill

Marinade:
1 cup extra dry vermouth
2 cups salad oil
2 teaspoons lemon juice
2 medium onions
4 garlic cloves, minced
2 teaspoons chopped basil
2 teaspoons salt
4 peppercorns, crushed

4-8 rib rack of lamb or
   lamb chops
4 link sausages or chicken
   or beef wieners
4 lamb kidneys or chicken
   livers
8 mushrooms
8 pieces green pepper
8 pieces sweet red pepper
4 cherry tomatoes

Marinade: Combine all ingredients in first column.
Pour marinade over the rack of lamb or lamb chops and marinate for several hours. Grill the meat, basting with the marinade. Parboil the sausages for 3 minutes, drain, and dry. Marinate the sausages or wieners and the kidneys or chicken livers for 1 hour. (Remove the fat and veins from the center of the lamb kidneys.) Arrange the meats and vegetables on 4 skewers. Brush well with the marinade and grill until browned.

Serves 4.

Irish Stew

3 pounds lamb neck or lamb
   shoulder chops, trimmed of
   fat, bone, & gristle
2 pounds potatoes, peeled
   & sliced

1 pound onions, peeled
   & sliced
1 tablespoon chopped parsley
1 teaspoon dried thyme
1½-2 cups water
Salt and pepper

Cut the trimmed meat into fairly large pieces. Place a layer of potatoes in a pan, then the herbs, then the sliced meat, and finally the onions. Season each layer well and repeat this once more, finishing with a thick layer of potatoes. Pour the water over, cover with a sheet of foil, then the lid, and either bake at 250° or simmer very gently on top of the stove, shaking from time to time so that it does not stick, for about 2 hours. Add a little more liquid if the stew seems to be getting very dry.

Serves 6 to 8.

Baked Lamb Shoulder Steaks

6 lamb shoulder steaks
1 teaspoon salt
¼ teaspoon pepper
½ teaspoon paprika
6 tablespoons butter
1 (#303) can artichoke
   hearts, drained

¼ pound mushrooms, sliced
2 tablespoons flour
1 cup chicken broth
¼ cup white cooking wine
½ teaspoon rosemary,
   crumbled

Sprinkle the lamb steaks with salt, pepper, and paprika. Brown in 4 tablespoons butter and place in a casserole or baking dish so that the steaks fit in a single layer. Arrange the artichoke hearts around the steaks. Add 2 tablespoons butter to the drippings and sauté the mushrooms. Sprinkle the flour over the mushrooms and stir in the broth, wine, and rosemary. Cook until thickened. Pour over the steaks. Cover and bake at 375° for 45 minutes to 1 hour, according to the thickness of the steak.

Serves 6.

Pork

Pork Sauerkraut Casserole

6 pork steaks, ¾-inch thick
1 (32 ounce) jar sauerkraut
1 cup chopped onion
4 tart apples, chopped

1 ½ teaspoons caraway seeds
2 tablespoons horseradish-
  mustard mixture or 1 ½
  tablespoons horseradish &
  ¼ teaspoon dry mustard

Brown the pork steaks in some of the fat trimmed from them. Place in a large casserole or baking dish. Combine and add to the pork steaks all remaining ingredients. Cover and bake at 350° for 1 hour.

Serves 6.

Baked Country Style Spareribs

4 pounds spareribs or
  2-2½ pounds country-style
  spareribs
2 tablespoons Worcestershire
  sauce
2 tablespoons vinegar
2 tablespoons brown sugar
1 ½ teaspoons salt

1 teaspoon chili powder,
  or to taste
¼ teaspoon pepper
1 medium onion, chopped
1 clove garlic, crushed
  or minced
¾ cup catusp
1 ½ cups water

Cut the spareribs between the bones to make individual ribs or use country-style spareribs. Place the ribs in a single layer in a large shallow pan and bake at 350° for 30 minutes. Meanwhile, combine the Worcestereshire sauce, vinegar, brown sugar, salt, chili powder, pepper, onion, garlic, catsup, and water. Bring this mixture to a boil and simmer 5 minutes. Remove from the heat. Drain the excess fat from the ribs. Pour the warm sauce over the ribs. Bake for about 1 hour, turning and basting occasionally with the sauce in the pan.

Serve with rice, mashed potatoes, or spaghetti and a green salad.

Serves 4.

131

Pork Chops with Wine

8 thinly sliced, center-cut
   pork chops
Salt & pepper
1 tablespoon butter
1 tablespoon olive oil

1 cup Pinot Noir or
   dry red wine
1 clove garlic, crushed
1 tablespoon tomato paste
½ cup canned consommé,
   undiluted
Chopped parsley

Season the pork chops with salt and pepper. Brown in the butter and olive oil, about 5 minutes on each side. Add the wine, garlic, tomato paste, and consommé. Cook about 5 minutes longer. Sprinkle generously with chopped parsley and serve immediately.

This is delicious served with mashed potatoes, steamed carrots, a wedge of lettuce with bleu cheese, or applesauce.

Serves 4.

Sweet-Sour Spareribs

5 pounds pork spareribs,
   cut in pieces or
   country-style spareribs
1 cup golden brown
   sugar, packed
3 tablespoons cornstarch
1 tablespoon dry mustard

1 cup vinegar
1 cup crushed pineapple,
   undrained
¾ cup catsup
¾ cup water
¼ cup finely chopped onion
3 tablespoons soy sauce

Spread the ribs in a single layer in a large shallow pan. Brown at 425° for 20-30 minutes; drain off the fat. Combine the sugar, cornstarch, and mustard in a saucepan. Add the remaining ingredients; mix well. Cook over medium heat until thick and glossy, stirring constantly. Spoon half the sauce over the ribs. Reduce the heat to 350° and bake 45 minutes. Turn the ribs, cover with the remaining sauce, and bake 30 minutes or until well done.

Makes 6 servings.

Sausage & Potato Pie

1 pound pre-browned tiny
  sausages
3 large eggs
½ cup milk
½ cup coarsely grated
  Swiss cheese

½ cup chopped onion
1 pound frozen hash brown
  potatoes, thawed
Chopped parsley

Grease a 1-inch deep-dish pie plate. Place the sausages in a spoke wheel design in the pie plate, or cut the sausages in small pin wheels and scatter over the plate. Beat the eggs in a large bowl; add the milk, cheese, onion, and potatoes. Spoon over the sausages. Bake at 375° for 30-35 minutes, until the mixture is set and is lightly browned. Remove from the oven and let stand 5-10 minutes. Sprinkle with parsley and serve.

Serves 4.

Mexican Style Pork Stew

2 pounds boneless
  pork shoulder,
  cut into 1-inch cubes
1 tablespoon shortening
2-3 tablespoons flour
1½ teaspoons chili powder
2 teaspoons salt
1 clove garlic, minced

1 cup water
1 (1 pound) can tomato
  wedges, undrained
1 (1 pound) can small, whole
  white potatoes, drained
1 cup celery chunks,
  cut into 1-inch pieces
2 medium-size onions,
  quartered

Brown the pork cubes on all sides in the hot shortening in a Dutch oven over moderate heat, stirring as needed to brown evenly. Stir in the flour, chili powder, 1 teaspoon salt, and garlic. Add the water; cover and cook over low heat about 1 hour or until the meat is almost tender. Add the vegetables and remaining 1 teaspoon salt. Cover; cook 15-20 minutes or until the meat and vegetables are tender.

Serves 4 to 6.

133

Barbecued Pork Chops

8 (1-inch) rib pork chops
Flour
¼ cup shortening
2 tablespoons flour
2 tablespoons prepared
    mustard
¼ cup chopped onion
½ teaspoon cloves

1 teaspoon salt
½ teaspoon pepper
2 tablespoons Worcestershire
    sauce
1 cup juice from peach, apple,
    bread & butter, or sweet
    pickles
1 cup catsup

Dredge the chops in flour and then brown in hot shortening. Pour off all excess fat. Add the 2 tablespoons flour to the mustard to make a paste. Add the remaining ingredients. Blend well and pour over the chops. Cover and simmer slowly for 1½ hours.

Serves 8.

Intoxicated Pork Chops

8 thinly sliced, center cut
    pork chops
1 tablespoon butter
1 tablespoon olive oil
Salt & pepper to taste
1 cup Marsala or other
    dry red wine

1 clove garlic, crushed
1 tablespoon tomato paste
    or catsup
½ cup condensed canned
    consommé or seasoned
    bouillon
Parsley

Brown the chops in butter and olive oil for about 5 minutes on each side. Season with salt and pepper. Add the Marsala wine, garlic, tomato paste or catsup, and the consommé or bouillon. Cook about 5 minutes longer. Sprinkle generously with chopped parsley and serve immediately.

Serves 4.

Roman Pork Chops

6 pork chops, ½-inch thick
Oil
½ teaspoon salt
¼ teaspoon pepper
2 (1 pound) cans whole
   tomatoes

1 (4 ounce) jar button
   mushroom, liquid reserved
½ cup chopped green pepper
¼ cup instant minced onion
8 ounces enriched durum
   thin spaghetti
6 slices sharp cheddar cheese

Brown the chops in oil. Season with salt and pepper. Add the tomatoes, mushrooms and liquid, green pepper, and onion. Cover and simmer 25 minutes. Add the spaghetti and continue cooking 20 minutes, or until the chops and spaghetti are tender. During the last few minutes of cooking, top with slices of cheese cut into triangles.

Serves 6.

Chinese Style Barbecued Pork

4 (½ pound) pork loins
½ cup sugar

1 tablespoon salt
1 cup soy sauce
2 tablespoons dry sherry wine

Prepare the pork loins by cutting into strips 7 inches long, 1½ inches wide, and 1¼ inches thick. Coat the pork strips with a mixture of sugar and salt. Let stand at room temperature for 1 hour. Mix the soy sauce and wine, and coat the pork strips thoroughly on all sides; let stand 45 minutes, turning the strips at least once. Place the marinated strips fat-side up on a wire rack in a foil-lined shallow pan. Roast at 500° for 15 minutes; reduce the oven temperature to 350° and continue cooking for 45 minutes or until the meat is done (internal temperature 180° on meat thermometer), turning the strips at least once. Remove from the oven. Cool slightly before slicing. Serve with Chinese-style hot mustard and toasted sesame seeds.

Serves 8 to 10.

Veal

Veal Piccata

½ cup flour
1 ½ pounds veal, sliced
⅛-inch thick*
6 tablespoons butter

1 teaspoon salt or to taste
½ cup dry white wine
Juice of ½ lemon
Sprigs of parsley

Flour the veal. Melt the butter over medium heat and add the veal slices. Turn the meat the minute the edges whiten and salt lightly. When both sides are done, pour in the wine, and let bubble until the vapors cease to tingle the nose. Add the lemon juice and stir gently with a wooden spoon. Serve with sprigs of parsley.

If the veal from the market comes thicker, lay it on a board and pound thinner with a meat mallet, then flour thoroughly.

Serves 4.

Veal Marsala

½ pound veal, thinly sliced
½ cup flour
¼ teaspoon salt
¼ teaspoon pepper
¼ teaspoon garlic salt

½ cup butter
2 tablespoons chopped onion
1 cup sliced mushrooms,
   fresh or canned
½ cup Marsala (dry red wine)

Cut the veal into 2 servings. Mix the flour with the salt, pepper, and garlic salt. Coat the veal with the flour mixture. Sauté in butter, browning on both sides. Slide the veal to the skillet's edge. Add the onions and mushrooms. Stir and cook. Add the wine; simmer a few minutes.

Serves 2.

Chinese Veal

1½ pounds veal shoulder,
   diced
2 medium onions, chopped
½ cup rice, uncooked
1 can chicken and rice soup

¼ cup soy sauce
1 cup hot water
1 cup diced celery
1 package frozen peas
Slivered almonds

Brown the veal in a skillet with the chopped onions. Place the mixture in a greased casserole. Add the rice, soup, soy sauce, and water. Cover and bake at 425° for 40 minutes. Remove from the oven and add the celery and peas. Return to the oven and cook, covered, for 20 minutes longer. Garnish with slivered almonds.

Serves 6 to 8.

Veal Supreme

8 veal steaks
½ cup plus 1 tablespoon
   olive oil
1½ tablespoons wine vinegar
¼ teaspoon oregano
¼ teaspoon sweet basil
1 large onion, finely chopped
1 large carrot, finely chopped
3 stalks celery, finely chopped
3-4 sprigs parsley, chopped

1 (4 ounce) can mushrooms,
   liquid reserved
Flour
2 eggs, beaten with
   2 tablespoons water
1-1½ cups fine dry
   bread crumbs
1 teaspoon salt
½ teaspoon pepper
1 cup tomato juice
½ cup dry sherry

One hour before cooking, marinate, for about ½ hour, the veal steaks in 3 tablespoons of olive oil, the wine vinegar, oregano, and basil. Dip the drained and dried steaks in flour, then in the egg-water mixture. Finally, coat both sides of the veal steaks with the fine dry read crumbs. Place the steaks on a rack and allow to dry for ½ hour. Heat 6 tablespoons of olive oil in a large, heavy skillet. Brown the veal over medium heat until golden. Remove the meat to a warm platter. Add to the skillet the chopped onion, carrot, celery, parsley, and mushrooms, drained. Season with salt and pepper. Sauté over low heat, stirring often. Add the tomato juice, sherry, and mushroom liquid. Cook about 5 minutes. Return the meat to the skillet; cover. Simmer about ½ hour or until tender.

Serves 8.

Casseroles

Rice and Seafood Casserole

2 packages long grain
  and wild rice
¼ cup butter
1 onion, finely chopped
¾ pound medium-size
  mushrooms
Juice of ½ lemon
2 tablespoons flour
1 ¼ cups (1 can) chicken stock
½ cup dry white wine
½ teaspoon salt

¼ teaspoon garlic salt
¼ teaspoon crumbled
  dry tarragon
3 tablespoons grated
  Parmesan cheese
½ pound medium-size
  shrimp, cooked
⅓ pound (1 can) crab meat
1 tablespoon finely
  chopped parsley

Cook the rice according to package directions; however, do not use the seasoning packet in the package. This will take about 25 minutes from start to finish. Meanwhile, melt 2 tablespoons butter in a large frying pan. Add the onion and sauté until golden. Wash the mushrooms and pull out the stems, leaving the caps whole. Add the mushroom caps and stems to the pan, and sprinkle with lemon juice. Cook gently, stirring occasionally, until the mushrooms are tender. In a saucepan, melt 2 tablespoons butter, blend in the flour, mixing to make a roux. Pour in the chicken stock and wine. Cook, stirring until thickened. Add the salt, garlic salt, tarragon, and Parmesan cheese. Mix together ¾ of the sauce, rice, mushrooms, shrimp, and crab meat, reserving some shrimp and crab for garnish. Spoon into a buttered 2 quart casserole. Arrange the reserved seafood on top, and spoon on the remaining sauce. Cover and bake at 350° for 20 minutes or 30-35 minutes if the casserole was refrigerated. Sprinkle with parsley just before serving.

Serves 6 to 8.

Chicken & Rice - Spanish Style

1 (2½-3 pound) fryer chicken
½ cup flour
1½ teaspoons salt
1 teaspoon paprika
½ teaspoon pepper
¼ cup olive oil
¼ cup finely chopped
   green onions
¼ cup finely chopped
   yellow Spanish onions
½ small clove garlic,
   finely chopped
1 cup peeled, seeded,
   & chopped tomatoes
2 cups hot chicken broth
   or bouillon

1½ teaspoons salt
¼ teaspoon pepper
Small piece of bay leaf
1 whole clove
⅛ teaspoon powdered saffron,
   optional
2 tablespoons finely
   chopped parsley
1 cup regular long-grain rice
1 small green pepper, slivered
2 tablespoons chopped
   pimento
⅓ cup fresh or frozen peas
¼ cup dry sherry

Rinse the chicken and pat dry. Combine the flour, salt, paprika, and pepper in a paper or plastic bag. Shake the chicken pieces, 2 or 3 at a time, to coat lightly. Heat the olive oil in a large, heavy skillet and add the chicken. Brown slowly on all sides. Push the chicken to one side of the skillet and add the green onions, yellow Spanish onions, and garlic. Cook, stirring gently, for 3 minutes. Spread the chicken pieces out in the skillet. Add the tomatoes, chicken broth, salt, pepper, bay leaf, clove, powdered saffron, parsley, and rice. Bring the liquid to a boil. Lower the heat and sprinkle in the green pepper and pimento. Cover tightly, and simmer 30 minutes or until the chicken and rice are tender. Add the peas the last 5 minutes of cooking. Stir in the sherry.

Serves 4.

Chicken and Zucchini Skillet

1 tablespoon butter
6-8 small zucchini,
    unpeeled & sliced
1 (2½-3 pound) fryer, cut-up
Salt and pepper

⅔ cup barbecue sauce
1 teaspoon dried
    oregano leaves
1 tablespoon lemon juice
1 teaspoon instant
    minced onion

Grease the bottom of a large covered skillet with the butter. Arrange the zucchini slices over the bottom. Sprinkle the fryer with salt and pepper. Place the chicken skin side up over the zucchini. In a small bowl, combine the barbecue sauce, oregano leaves, lemon juice, and minced onion and pour evenly over the chicken. Cover and simmer the chicken for 30 minutes, basting the chicken with sauce from the bottom of the skillet. Uncover. Continue cooking 10-20 minutes or until the chicken is tender. Baste frequently.

Serves 4.

Creole Meatballs & Noodles

1 pound ground beef
1 cup herb seasoned
    bread stuffing
½ cup canned applesauce
1 teaspoon salt
¼ teaspoon pepper
¼ cup cooking oil
1 cup sliced onions

½ cup sliced green pepper
1 clove garlic, minced
1 (6 ounce) can tomato paste
1 cup water
1 teaspoon oregano
1 (8 ounce) package
    wide noodles
Parmesan cheese, grated

Combine the ground beef, bread stuffing, canned applesauce, salt, and pepper. Mix well. Shape into 16 balls (about ¼ cup each). Sauté in the cooking oil. Push the browned meat to one side. Add the onions, green pepper, and garlic. Sauté until the vegetables are softened. Add the tomato paste, 1 cup water, and oregano. Cover and simmer 15-20 minutes. Meantime, cook the noodles. Serve the meat and sauce over hot noodles. Sprinkle with Parmesan cheese.

Serves 6.

Cheese Potato Casserole

6 cups sliced cooked potatoes
2 cups shredded cheddar
   cheese

2 large eggs, beaten
1 ½ cups milk
2 teaspoons salt
⅛-¼ teaspoon nutmeg

Layer half the potatoes and half the cheese in a shallow, buttered 2 quart casserole. Repeat the layers. Combine the eggs, milk, salt, and nutmeg. Pour the egg mixture over the potatoes and cheese. Bake at 350° for 35-40 minutes or until a knife inserted near the center comes out clean. Let stand 10 minutes before serving.

Serves 8.

Top of Stove Casserole

2½ cups split peas
2½ cups water
2 teaspoons salt
1 tablespoon butter
   or margarine
1 cup chopped onion

1 pound ground beef
2 cups (1 pound) canned
   tomatoes
½ cup uncooked rice
1 tablespoon sugar
¼ teaspoon pepper

Wash and place the split peas into a 2½ quart saucepan. Add 2 cups water and ½ teaspoon salt. Bring to a boil, uncovered, for 2 minutes. Remove from heat. Cover and let soak for ½ hour. In the meantime, place the butter in a skillet. Add the onion and sauté until golden in color. Add the ground beef. Stir and sauté until the color changes. Add the tomatoes, rice, ½ cup water, sugar, 1½ teaspoons salt, pepper, and split peas with liquid. Simmer 25-30 minutes or until the rice and peas are cooked, stirring occasionally. Correct the seasoning to taste. This casserole is delicious served with romaine salad and muffins.

Serves 6.

Steak Skillet Dinner

1 ½ pounds beef or
  calf round steak
⅓ cup flour
2-3 tablespoons vegetable oil
1 large onion, chopped
1 (16 ounce) can whole
  potatoes
¼ cup hamburger relish
1 tablespoon Worcestershire
  sauce

2 teaspoons bell pepper flakes
1 teaspoon instant beef
  bouillon
1 teaspoon salt
½ teaspoon dried
  marjoram leaves
¼ teaspoon pepper
1 (10 ounce) package frozen
  Italian green beans
1 (2 ounce) jar sliced pimento

Cut the steak into 4-6 serving pieces. Coat with the flour, then pound the flour into the beef. Brown the beef in vegetable oil in a large (10-inch) skillet. Push the beef to one side; add the chopped onion (about 1 cup). Cook and stir until tender, then drain. Drain and reserve the liquid from the canned potatoes, then add water to measure 1 cup liquid. Mix the potato liquid, hamburger relish, Worcestershire sauce, bell pepper flakes, beef bouillon, salt, marjoram leaves, and pepper. Pour over the beef and onion. Heat to boiling, then reduce heat. Cover and simmer until the beef is tender, 1¼ to 1½ hours. Rinse the green beans under running cold water to separate. Add the potatoes, beans, and pimento to the skillet. Heat to boiling, then reduce heat. Cover and simmer until the beans are tender, 10-15 minutes.

Serves 4 to 6.

Easy Summer Casserole

1 can condensed cream of
  chicken soup
½ cup milk
2 cups cooked noodles
1 cup cooked peas

2 cans boned chicken or
  turkey, cut up
2 slices (about 2 ounces)
  process cheese, cut into
  triangles

Blend the soup with the milk in a 1½-quart casserole. Mix in the cooked noodles, peas, and chicken or turkey. Bake at 400° for 20 minutes. Top with triangles of cheese. Bake until the cheese melts.

Serves 4.

Two, Two, Two Casserole

2 medium onions, chopped
2 tablespoons butter
2 pounds ground beef
2 teaspoons lemon pepper
    seaoning or seasoning salt

2 cans celery soup
2 pounds frozen, shredded,
    seasoned, & deep fried
    potato bits

Cook the onions in the butter until clear. Add the ground beef and cook until brown. Add the seasoning. Stir in the celery soup (do not add liquid). Fold in the frozen potato bits. Bake in a greased casserole at 350° for 1 hour.

Serves 6 to 8.

Cheese-Egg Bake

⅓ cup chopped onion
¼ pound fresh mushrooms,
    sliced
⅓ cup butter
¼ cup flour
1 teaspoon salt
1 teaspoon dry mustard
⅛ teaspoon pepper

3 cups milk
2 cups shredded sharp
    cheddar cheese
1 (10 ounce) package
    frozen peas
4 hard-boiled eggs, sliced
2 cups prepared biscuit mix

Sauté the onion and mushrooms in butter. Blend in the flour, salt, dry mustard, and pepper. Add 2⅓ cups milk. Cook, stirring constantly, until smooth and thickened. Add ½ cup shredded cheddar cheese. Stir until melted. Cook the peas according to package directions; drain. Stir the peas into the cheese mixture and fold in the eggs. Pour into a greased, shallow 2 quart baking dish. Bake at 425° for 10 minutes. Combine the prepared biscuit mix and ½ cup shredded cheddar cheese. Stir in ⅔ cup milk. Pat out into a 9-inch circle on a lightly floured board. Cut into 8 wedges. Remove the casserole from the oven and top with the biscuit wedges. Bake until the biscuits are browned, 10-12 minutes. Remove from the oven. Sprinkle the biscuits with 1 cup shredded cheddar cheese. Bake until the cheese melts, about 1-2 minutes.

Serves 6 to 8.

Meatball Potatoes

1 pound ground beef
⅓ cup finely chopped onion
1 cup milk
1 egg
1 tablespoon snipped parsley
1 teaspoon salt

½ teaspoon Worcestershire
  sauce
⅛ teaspoon pepper
¼ cup shortening
1 (5.5 ounce) box sour cream
  & chive potatoes
2¼ cups boiling water

Mix the ground beef, onion, ⅓ cup milk, egg, parsley, salt, Worcester-shire sauce, and pepper. Shape into 16 balls. Heat the shortening in a 10-inch skillet until melted. Cook and stir the meatballs in the shorten-ing until brown. Remove the meatballs and drain fat from skillet. Empty the potatoes into the skillet. Sprinkle with the sour cream mix. Stir in the boiling water and ⅔ cup milk. Arrange the meatballs on the potatoes. Heat to boiling, then reduce heat. Cover and simmer until potatoes are tender, about 30 minutes.

Serves 4 to 6.

Baked Beans with Ham

1 pound dry Navy beans
1 onion, sliced
2 teaspoons salt
¼ teaspoon Tabasco sauce
¼ cup catsup

¼ cup light molasses
1 tablespoon vinegar
1 teaspoon dry mustard
3 pound smoked ham shank
6-8 canned pineapple slices

Cover the Navy beans with 6 cups water. Bring to boil and boil 2 minutes. Cover and let stand 1 hour. Add the sliced onion and salt; cook until tender. Drain, reserving 1½ cups liquid. Mix the liquid with the Tabasco, catsup, molasses, vinegar, and mustard. Put the ham shank in a 3 quart casserole or Dutch oven. Put the beans around the ham. Pour the liquid over the top. Cover and bake at 325° for 1½ hours. Remove the ham and put the beans back in the oven. Bake, uncovered, for 1 hour. Slice the meat; add to the beans with pineapple slices. Bake 30 minutes longer.

Serves 6 to 8.

Skillet Supper

1 pound ground beef
1 tablespoon shortening
½ teaspoon salt
1 (6 ounce) can tomato paste
2½ cups water
1 package spaghetti
    sauce mix

1 cup (4 ounces)
    long spaghetti,
    broken in pieces
½ pint (1 cup) cottage cheese
1½ cups shredded
    cheddar cheese

Brown the ground beef in the shortening in a large skillet (10-12-inch). Add the salt. Remove from heat. Push the meat to one side, and combine the tomato paste and water in the other side of the skillet. Stir in the spaghetti sauce mix until smooth. Thoroughly mix with the meat. Scatter the spaghetti pieces over the sauce mixture. Turn up the heat until the sauce is boiling. Spoon the cottage cheese over the mixture and top with the shredded cheddar cheese. Cover tightly and turn the heat low enough to just keep the mixture simmering. Cook 25 minutes or until the spaghetti is tender.

Serves 6 to 8.

Variations:
1. Spaghetti sauce mix with mushrooms may be substituted.
2. Fresh or canned mushrooms may be added.
3. 1 cup sliced celery may be cooked with the meat.
4. Up to 6 ounces of spaghetti may be used. Makes a thicker sauce, and may need more water.
5. If elbow macaroni is used, increase cooking time to 35-40 minutes.

Spanish Arroz con Pollo

2½-3 pound frying chicken,
cut up
5 tablespoons butter or
margarine
2 teaspoons salt
⅛ teaspoon pepper
½ teaspoon oregano
1 (1 pound) can tomato
wedges, undrained

1 medium onion, sliced
1 bay leaf
1 cup converted rice
1 (13¾ ounce) can
chicken broth
1 (10 ounce) package frozen
peas, thawed
¼ cup water
2 tablespoons flour

Brown the chicken fryer in 3 tablespoons butter or margarine in a 10-inch skillet. Sprinkle with 1 teaspoon salt, pepper, and oregano. Add the tomato wedges, onion, and bay leaf. Cover and cook over low heat until the chicken is tender, about 45 minutes. Remove the bay leaf. To prepare the rice, cook in 2 tablespoons butter or margarine in a sauce-pan until golden, stirring occasionally. Add water to 1 can of chicken broth to make 2½ cups liquid or use chicken bouillon to make the chicken broth. Add the liquid and ½ teaspoon salt to the rice. Bring to a boil. Cover and cook over low heat for 20 minutes. Stir in the peas. (To thaw peas, place package under running hot water.) Add another ½ teaspoon salt (less if seasoned bouillon is used). Cook until all liquid is absorbed, about 5 minutes. Arrange the chicken, tomato wedges, and onion on the rice. Blend the water with the flour. Stir into the pan drip-pings. Cook, stirring constantly, until the sauce is thickened. Spoon over the chicken and rice.

Serves 4.

Gala Beef on English Muffins

2 tablespoons butter
2 (2½ ounce) jars dried or
   chipped beef
1 tablespoon flour
½ cup dry white wine
1 pint sour cream

2 tablespoons grated
   Parmesan cheese
1 (10-ounce) can artichoke
   hearts, thinly sliced
English muffins
Paprika

Melt the butter in a skillet over low heat. Add the dried or chipped beef, torn into bite-size pieces, and frizzle. Sprinkle with the flour and mix. Add the wine and sour cream. Stir in thoroughly until smooth. Add the Parmesan cheese and artichoke hearts. Stir gently, keeping heat low. When ready to serve, spoon over the English muffins, split, toasted, and buttered. Sprinkle with a touch of paprika.

Serves 4 to 6.

Salmon, Ham or Chicken Cheese Pie

½ cup mayonnaise
½ cup milk
2 eggs
1 tablespoon cornstarch
½ cup flaked salmon,
   cubed cooked ham, or
   chicken bits

1½ cups shredded
   Swiss cheese
⅓ cup sliced green onions or
   dry onions
Dash pepper
1 (9-inch) pie shell, unbaked

Mix together the mayonnaise, milk, eggs, and cornstarch until smooth. Stir in the salmon, ham, or chicken, Swiss cheese, onions, and pepper. Turn into the prepared pastry shell. Bake at 350° for 35-40 minutes or until golden brown on top and a knife inserted in the center comes out clean.

Serves 6 to 8.

Crabmeat and Mushrooms in Wine Sauce

¼ pound mushrooms, sliced
¼ cup butter
3 tablespoons flour
½ cup milk
½ cup dry white wine

½ teaspoon dry mustard
¼ teaspoon dried tarragon
Salt & pepper
1 can snow crab or shrimp
Buttered crumbs
Paprika

Sauté the mushrooms in butter for 3-4 minutes. Stir in the flour. When well blended, gradually add the milk and wine. Stir constantly until thick and smooth. Add the dry mustard, tarragon, salt and pepper to taste. Gently fold in the snow crab or shrimp. Pour into a casserole. Top with buttered crumbs. Dust with paprika and bake at 350° for 30 minutes.

Serves 4 to 6.

Quick and Easy Potato Casserole

1 can cream of celery soup
1 (3 ounce) package
   cream cheese
¼ cup fresh chopped onion
1 teaspoon salt

1 (12 ounce) package frozen
   hash-browned potatoes
1 cup shredded
   cheddar cheese
¼ teaspoon pepper

Combine the soup, cream cheese, and onion. Cook until the onion is tender and the cheese is melted. Add hash-browns (*I think country style are best*). Pour into a greased casserole, cover, and bake 45 minutes at 350° or until bubbly. Remove from the oven, sprinkle cheddar cheese over the top, and return to the oven until the cheese is melted and slightly brown. If it is too sloppy, remove the cover and cook for a few minutes more.

Wednesday's Casserole

1 (1 pound) can cut green
   beans or 2 cups cooked
   fresh green beans,
   reserving the juice
1 pound cottage cheese
1 egg, slightly beaten
1 tablespoon instant minced
   onion
¼ teaspoon salt

¼ cup grated Parmesan cheese
3 cups cooked rice
1 cup diced cooked beef or
   chicken
1 (6 ounce) can tomato paste
1 (8 ounce) can tomato sauce
½ teaspoon oregano
½ teaspoon sweet basil
2 tablespoons salad oil

Drain the green beans and save the liquid. Mix the cottage cheese with the egg, instant minced onion, salt, and Parmesan cheese. Place the cooked rice in a 2½ quart casserole. Top with the cottage cheese mixture, cooked beef or chicken, and green beans. Mix the tomato paste with ¾ cup reserved bean juice, tomato sauce, oregano, sweet basil, and salad oil. Pour over the beans. Bake at 375° for 30 minutes or until bubbly. Sprinkle with additional Parmesan cheese before serving.

I've also tried cut steamed zucchini in this recipe, and it's excellent. Use 2 cups.

Serves 6 to 8.

Beef Potato Yogurt Stroganoff

¾ cup chopped onions
4 tablespoons oil
1 pound hamburger
1 cup beef stock or bouillon

4½ cups sliced raw potatoes
   (about 3 pounds)
1½ teaspoons salt
¼ teaspoon pepper
Dash nutmeg
½ cup plain yogurt

Sauté the onions in oil. Add the hamburger and continue to sauté until the meat loses the red color. Add the beef stock, potatoes, salt, pepper, and nutmeg. Simmer gently for 30 minutes or until the potatoes are soft. Add the yogurt when the mixture is ready to be served.

Serves 6.

Western Casserole

1 (4 ounce) can green chiles,
   drained, seeded & diced
1 pound Monterey Jack
   cheese, shredded
1 pound cheddar
   cheese, shredded

4 eggs, separated
⅔ cup evaporated milk
1 tablespoon flour
½ teaspoon salt
⅛ teaspoon pepper
1 medium tomato
Parsley

Mix the chiles with the cheeses in a well-buttered 2 quart casserole. (If an extra-hot flavor is desired, use 2 cans green chiles.) Beat the egg whites to stiff peaks. Combine the egg yolks, evaporated milk, flour, salt, and pepper, and beat until well blended. Gently fold the beaten whites into the yolk mixture. Pour over the cheese and, using a fork, lift the cheese to let the egg mixture flow through. Bake at 325° for 30 minutes. Slice the tomatoes and arrange around the edge of a casserole, overlapping slices. Bake an additional 30 minutes or until a knife inserted in the center comes out clean. Garnish with additional chiles or parsley.
Serves 6 to 8.

Carry Aboard Casserole

1 onion, chopped
½ green pepper, chopped
1 pound ground beef
¼ pound butter
1 teaspoon salt
1 (4 ounce) can mushrooms
1 clove garlic, minced
1 (16 ounce) can
   creamed corn

2 (8 ounce) cans tomato
   sauce
1 cup tomato juice
1 (8-ounce) package
   wide noodles
1 cup grated sharp
   cheddar cheese
¼ cup ripe olives, sliced

Sauté the onion and green pepper with the ground beef in butter. Add the salt, mushrooms, garlic, creamed corn, tomato sauce, and tomato juice. Combine in a casserole. Add the cooked noodles. Sprinkle with the cheddar cheese. Garnish with the ripe olives. Bake at 350° for about 30 minutes or until hot and the cheese melts. If an oven is not available, heat slowly in a Dutch oven, stirring until the cheese melts and the casserole is hot.
Serves 4 to 6.

Swiss Cheese Pie

1 tablespoon soft butter or
  margarine
1 (9-inch) pie shell, chilled
12 slices bacon
4 eggs
2 cups heavy cream or
  evaporated milk

¾ teaspoon salt
Pinch nutmeg, sugar,
  & cayenne
⅛ teaspoon pepper
1 cup grated natural
  Swiss cheese

Rub the butter over the surface of the pie shell. Fry the bacon until crisp; crumble into small pieces. Combine the eggs, cream, salt, nutmeg, sugar, cayenne, and pepper using an egg beater; beat just long enough to mix thoroughly. Sprinkle the bacon and cheese into the shell; pour in the cream mixture. Bake at 425° for 15 minutes. Reduce heat to 300°; bake 40 minutes longer, or until a knife inserted in center comes out clean. (If desired, 6 slices of bacon may be saved for garnish. Cook until done, but not too crisp. Roll each slice and arrange with seam side down in a bed of parsley around the pie plate.) Serve at once, cut into wedges.

Makes 6 servings.

Tamale Pie

2 tablespoons fat
½ pound ground beef
1 green pepper, chopped
1 cup chopped onion
3 teaspoons seasoned salt
⅛ teaspoon pepper
1 (12 ounce) can whole
  kernel corn
1 (#2½ can) tomatoes

¼ teaspoon garlic powder
1-2 tablespoons chili powder
1 teaspoon salt
1 cup yellow corn meal
1 cup evaporated milk
2 eggs, beaten
1 cup pitted ripe olives, sliced
1½ cups grated sharp
  cheddar cheese

Heat the fat in a deep skillet or Dutch oven. Add the ground beef, green pepper, chopped onion, 1 teaspoon seasoned salt, and pepper, and sauté until the meat is lightly browned. Add the corn, tomatoes, garlic powder, chili powder, salt, and 2 teaspoons seasoned salt. Stir in the corn meal, milk, eggs, olives, and 1 cup grated cheese. Stir until well mixed. Pour into a greased 3 quart casserole dish. Top with ½ cup grated cheese. Sprinkle with paprika. Bake at 350° for about 1 hour.

Serves 6.

Soups

Innsbruck Bacon Dumpling Soup

⅓ cup minced onion
1 tablespoon butter
3 slices bacon, minced
4 cups diced, day-old
  French bread
¾ cup milk
1 egg
1 egg yolk

¼ cup flour
½ teaspoon salt
Pepper to taste
2 tablespoons minced parsley
6 cups hot consommé or
  beef broth
Snipped chives

In a skillet, sauté the onion in butter until it is softened; stir in the minced bacon and cook the mixture over moderate heat, stirring, until the bacon is translucent. Pour the mixture into a bowl over the diced bread. In a small bowl, combine the milk, egg, egg yolk, flour, salt, and pepper. Stir the mixture into the bacon mixture with the minced parsley and let the mixture stand, covered, for 1 hour. Mash the mixture with a wooden spoon and, with moistened hands, form it into 12 balls. Drop the balls into a kettle of lightly salted, simmering water and cook for 15 minutes, or until they are cooked through. Transfer the dumplings with a slotted spoon to a tureen, add hot consommé or broth, and sprinkle the soup generously with snipped chives.

Serves 4.

Today's Senate Bean Soup

2 pounds dry Navy beans
4 quarts hot water
1½ pounds smoked
  ham hocks

1 onion, chopped
1 tablespoon butter
Salt & pepper to taste

Rinse the beans in hot water. Combine the beans with 4 quarts hot water and the ham hocks. Boil slowly for about 3 hours in a covered pot. Braise the onion in butter, and when light brown, put in the bean soup. Season.

Serves 8.

Czechoslovakian Cabbage Soup

2 pounds beef neck bones
1 cup chopped onion
3 carrots, chopped
2 cloves garlic, minced
1 bay leaf
2 pounds beef short ribs
1 teaspoon thyme
½ teaspoon paprika
8 cups water

8 cups coarsely chopped
  cabbage
2 (1 pound) cans tomatoes
2 teaspoons salt
½ teaspoon Tabasco sauce
¼ cup chopped parsley
3 tablespoons lemon juice
3 tablespoons sugar
1 (1 pound) can sauerkraut,
  rinsed & drained
Sour cream

In a large roasting pan place the beef bones, onion, carrots, garlic, and bay leaf. Top with the short ribs and sprinkle with thyme and paprika. Roast, uncovered, at 450° for 20 minutes, or until the meat is brown. You may use this same pan on top of the stove if you like, or you may transfer all this to a large kettle. Add the water, cabbage, tomatoes, salt, and Tabasco. Bring to a boil, then cover and simmer 1½ hours. Skim off the fat. Take the short ribs and bones out now, and remove the meat from the bones and return to the kettle. Add the parsley, lemon juice, sugar, and sauerkraut. Cook, uncovered, at 450° for 1 hour. Serve with a dollop of sour cream. If made a day ahead, the flavor is increased.

Serves 10 to 12.

Sour Cream Chestnut Bisque

3 tablespoons butter
1 large stalk celery,
  finely chopped
1 large carrot, finely chopped
½ onion, finely chopped
48 ounces canned chicken
  broth, approximately
2 sprigs parsley

1 bay leaf
¼ teaspoon ground cloves
1 (10 ounce) can whole
  chestnuts, drained
1 (16 ounce) carton
  sour cream
¼ cup snipped parsley
Salt & pepper to taste

In a 4 quart saucepan, melt the butter. Stir in the celery, carrot, and

162

onion. Cover and cook over low heat 10 minutes. Stir in the chicken broth, parsley, bay leaf, and cloves. Simmer 20 minutes. Crumble the chestnuts and stir into the broth. Simmer 3 minutes. Pour 3 cups into a blender container; cover and puree. Pour into a 3 quart saucepan. Repeat until all the broth is pureed. Stir in the sour cream and snipped parsley. Add salt and pepper to taste. Heat over low heat until warm. Do not boil because the sour cream will curdle.

Makes 8 (1 cup) servings.

Maui 7-Bean Soup

3 smoked ham hocks
1 pound soup bones
1 cup navy beans
⅔ cup pinto beans
⅔ cup cranberry beans
⅔ cup kidney beans
⅔ cup black eye beans

⅔ cup garbanzo beans
⅔ cup lima beans
5 medium onions
5 medium carrots
5 stalks celery
1 (#2½) can solid pack
    tomatoes
1 hot garlic sausage

Cover the ham hocks and soup bones with water; add half again as much water. Simmer, covered, for 2½ hours. During the same time, simmer the navy, pinto, cranberry, kidney, black eye, garbanzo, and lima beans in water, covered, for about 2 hours or until tender. If needed, add more water. *(I prefer to soak the dry beans overnight.)* Meantime, finely chop the onions, carrots, and celery. Add to the meat stock after it has cooked 2½ hours. Cut the meat into bite-size pieces and add the cooked beans and tomatoes. Cut the garlic sausage in slices, about ¼-inch thick, and pan-fry until lightly browned. Add to the soup. Slowly simmer for about 30 minutes. The soup should be cooled with ventilation under the pot. Refrigerate.

This soup should be cooked a day before serving and gets better as it ages. If it lasts for more than a couple of days, add finely shredded cabbage or pumpkin the last time around.

Serves 8 to 10.

Katherine's Favorite Chicken Soup

5 pounds chicken,
  bony pieces
2 quarts water
1 onion, halved
1 carrot, quartered
1 stalk celery, quartered
1 small white turnip,
  quartered

2 tablespoons dry sherry wine
Few sprigs parsley
1 clove garlic
1 bay leaf
1 slice lemon
2 teaspoons salt
½ teaspoon dried thyme
  leaves or 1 sprig fresh thyme
10 peppercorns

In a 6-8 quart pot, bring all the ingredients to a boil over moderately high heat. Reduce the heat to low, cover the pot, leaving lid slightly ajar, and simmer 2-3 hours. Strain the broth into 1 or more containers; reserve the vegetables and bones. Remove the meat from the bones; discard the skin and bones. Slice the vegetables. Cover the broth, meat, and vegetables, and refrigerate. To serve: skim and discard the fat from the top of the chilled broth. Reheat the broth with the meat and vegetables.

Makes about 6 cups.

Quick Trick Clam Chowder

1 (5½ ounce) package
  scalloped potatoes mix
Milk
1 (7-8 ounce) can minced
  clams

1 tablespoon minced
  green onion
1 tablespoon freeze-dried
  green pepper
2½ cups milk
1 tablespoon butter

In a large saucepan mix the potato slices, seasoned sauce mix, and the amounts of water and milk called for on the package. Add the liquid drained from the clams, green onion, and green pepper. Heat to boiling, stirring occasionally. Reduce heat; cover and simmer, stirring occasionally, about 25 minutes or until potatoes are tender. Stir in the clams, milk, and butter. Heat through.

Makes 6 (1 cup) servings.

Puget Sound Chowder

¼ pound diced salt pork
¼ pound diced bacon
1 cup diced onion
1 cup carrots
2½ cups diced raw potatoes
¼ cup diced celery
1 small clove garlic
Small piece bay leaf
¼ teaspoon crushed
  rosemary

¼ teaspoon crushed basil
½ teaspoon crushed thyme
3 peppercorns
1½ teaspoons salt
1 tablespoon Worcestershire
  sauce
1 quart cleaned,
  chopped clams
1 quart clam liquor & water
1 quart rich milk or cream

Brown the salt pork and bacon until crisp. Set the bacon and salt pork aside. Carefully fry the diced onion until delicately browned. Add the diced carrots, raw potatoes, celery, and garlic; cover and simmer 10 minutes. Add the seasonings. Add the bacon and salt pork, clams, clam liquor, and water; stir and mix well. Cook gently until the vegetables and clams are cooked. Add the rich milk or cream; stir to combine all. Heat to serve, but do not boil.

Serves 6 to 8.

Senate Bean Soup (1872)

3 cups dry Navy beans
4½ quarts water
1 ham bone
1½ pounds smoked pork
¾ teaspoon celery salt

1½ tablespoons minced onion
⅓ teaspoon dry mustard
Salt & pepper to taste
Chopped parsley

Soak the beans in water to cover overnight. Drain. Add the water, ham bone, pork, celery salt, and onion. Cook the beans until very soft. Remove the bone and smoked pork and dice the meat. Press the remaining bean mixture through a coarse colander or cream thoroughly with a wooden spoon. Combine with the meat, adding mustard, salt, and pepper. Heat to boiling, stirring. Garnish with parsley.

Serves 8 to 10.

Shirley's Ground Beef Soup

1 pound lean ground beef
1 cup diced onion
1 cup cubed raw potatoes
1 cup sliced carrots
1 cup shredded cabbage
½ cup diced celery
1 (16 ounce) can tomatoes

6 cups water
¼ cup rice or pearl barley
1 small bay leaf
½ teaspoon thyme
½ teaspoon rosemary
½ teaspoon sweet basil
4 teaspoons salt
½ teaspoon pepper

Brown the ground beef and onion in a moderately hot skillet or Dutch oven, stirring and cooking until the color changes. Add the potatoes, carrots, cabbage, celery, tomatoes, and the water. Bring to a boil. Sprinkle in the rice or pearl barley, bay leaf, thyme, rosemary, sweet basil, salt, and pepper. Stir to blend all ingredients. Simmer gently for 1 hour, stirring occasionally.

Excellent reheated!

Serves 6.

Hearty Tuna Cheese Chowder

4 tablespoons butter
¼ cup chopped celery
1 cup chopped onion
1 cup diced potato
1¼ teaspoon salt
¼ teaspoon white pepper
½ teaspoon thyme, crumbled
¼ teaspoon dill weed

2 tablespoons flour
1 (8 ounce) can stewed
   tomatoes
3 cups milk
1 (6½-7 ounce) can tuna,
   drained
2 tablespoons minced parsley
1 cup grated Monterey Jack
   cheese

Combine 2 tablespoons butter, celery, onion, and potato. Cook over medium heat for 14 minutes, stirring often until the potato is tender. Stir in the salt, pepper, thyme, dill, and flour. Add the tomatoes, milk, tuna, and parsley. Heat, stirring until the soup is thickened and boils. Stir in the cheese and remaining 2 tablespoons butter.

Menu suggestion: Serve with spinach salad, French bread, cake, and milk.

Makes 5 cups (4 dinner servings).

Barbecued Pork Noodle Soup

1 pound fine Chinese noodles
Seasoning salt
1 (10½ ounce) can chicken
   broth, undiluted
1 can water
Salt & pepper

1 drop sesame oil
¼ pound barbecued pork,
   sliced
½ can water chestnuts, sliced
3 green onions with tops,
   sliced
1 hard-boiled egg, sliced

Cook the noodles in salted water until tender. Drain and season with seasoning salt to taste. Combine the chicken broth, water, and salt and pepper to taste. Add sesame oil. Adjust the seasoning. Serve the noodles in Chinese bowls. Add the broth and garnish with barbecued pork, water chestnuts, green onions, and egg. Serve with chopsticks and a Chinese soup spoon. Serve hot.

Note: Other cooked meats and chicken may be used instead of the barbecued pork.

Serve 4 to 6.

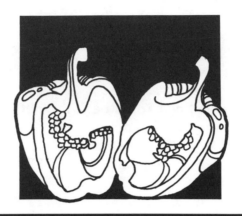

Vegetables

Asparagus Cheese Casserole

3 slices bread
3 tablespoons sharp cheese
   spread
2½ cups cut, cooked asparagus
   or 2 packages frozen cut
   asparagus
2 tablespoons butter
2 tablespoons flour

1 cup milk or
   asparagus liquid
1 can cream of mushroom
   soup, undiluted
½ teaspoon salt
⅔ cup buttered bread crumbs
2 asparagus spears
1 thin slice pimento

Spread the bread with the cheese; cut into ½-inch cubes. Combine the cubes with asparagus in a greased 1½ quart casserole. Melt the butter in a small saucepan; blend in the flour. Add the milk, and cook until thick, stirring constantly. Add the soup and salt. Combine this sauce with the asparagus mixture. Top with buttered bread crumbs. Bake at 350° for about 15 minutes or until crumbs are brown. Garnish with 2 asparagus spears and a slice of pimento.

Serves 8.

Baked Broccoli & Cheese

1 pound fresh broccoli or
   2 (10 ounce) packages
   frozen broccoli
3 eggs
1 cup evaporated milk

1 teaspoon instant minced
   onion
½ teaspoon salt
Dash pepper
1½ cups shredded sharp
   cheddar cheese

Cook either fresh or frozen broccoli in a small amount of boiling water until barely tender. Drain and put in a shallow 1½ quart baking dish. Beat the eggs and stir in the remaining ingredients. Pour over the broccoli. Set the dish in a pan of hot water and bake at 350° for about 30 minutes or until set.

Serves 4 to 6.

171

Broccoli Casserole Parmesan

1 quart salted water
2 bunches broccoli, washed
½ cup grated Parmesan
   cheese

Cream Sauce:
2 tablespoons melted butter
2 tablespoons flour
¼ teaspoon salt
⅛ teaspoon white pepper
⅓ cup milk
⅔ cup light cream

Bring the salted water to boil in a saucepan. Add the broccoli and boil, covered, for 15 minutes. Drain the broccoli in a colander. Cut in 2-inch pieces, discarding any woody stems. Place in a 2 quart casserole. Pour the **Cream Sauce** over the broccoli. Sprinkle with Parmesan cheese. Bake at 350° for 15 minutes. Place under the broiler for 2 minutes or until brown.

Cream Sauce: In a saucepan, make a paste of the melted butter, flour, and seasonings. Add the milk and light cream all at once, and stir continually over low heat, until the sauce thickens.

Serves 6.

Brussels Sprouts with Celery

3 tablespoons butter or
   margarine
2 cups thinly sliced celery
½ cup finely chopped onion
3 tablespoons flour
1 teaspoon celery salt

1 (13¾-14 ounce) can or jar
   chicken broth
1 pound fresh Brussels sprouts
   or 2 (10 ounce) packages
   frozen Brussels sprouts
Parsley, chopped (optional)

Melt the butter in a large saucepan over low heat. Stir in the celery and onion; cook until just tender. Stir in the flour, celery salt, and chicken broth. Cook, stirring constantly, until the sauce thickens. Add the Brussels sprouts, cooked and drained. Heat thoroughly. Place in a serving dish. Sprinkle with chopped parsley if desired.

Serves 6 to 8.

172

Noodles & Cabbage

8 ounces broad noodles
4 tablespoons butter
3 tablespoons flour
2 cups milk

1 cup diced sharp
  cheddar cheese
3 cups finely shredded cabbage
1 cup dry bread crumbs
¼ cup melted butter

Cook the noodles in boiling, salted water until tender. Drain. Melt the butter in a saucepan and add the flour. Stir until smooth. Add the milk and continue to stir and cook until smooth and thick. Lower the heat and add the cheddar cheese. Stir until thoroughly blended. In a buttered casserole, alternate a layer of cabbage, the noodles, and the cheese sauce. Make 2 layers. Combine the bread crumbs with the melted butter. Sprinkle over the top of the casserole. Bake at 375° for 35 minutes.

Serves 6.

Rice-Carrot Casserole

2 eggs, well beaten
1¼ cups milk
1 tablespoon grated onion
½ teaspoon salt
⅛ teaspoon pepper

1 tablespoon melted butter
  or margarine
2 cups shredded carrots
2 cups shredded cheddar
  cheese
2 cups cooked rice

Mix together the eggs, milk, grated onion, salt, pepper, and butter or margarine. Stir in the carrots, cheese, and rice. Mix thoroughly. Turn into a deep 1½ quart casserole. Cover and bake at 350° for 20 minutes; uncover and bake 40 minutes longer. Let stand 10 minutes before serving.

Serves 6.

Onion Crispy

4 Bermuda or sweet white
  onions
2 tablespoons butter

6 slices bread
2 tablespoons mayonnaise
2 cups grated cheddar cheese

Parboil the onions in salted water for 5 minutes. Cool and cut into ⅜-inch thick slices. Separate into rings. Butter a 13½x8¾x 1¾-inch baking dish, a jelly roll pan, or shallow baking pan. Butter the bread and spread with mayonnaise. Place in the baking dish. Cover the bread with the onion rings. Sprinkle with the cheese. Bake at 350° for 30 minutes.

This is excellent served with broiled hamburgers, steak, or grilled dishes.

Serves 4 to 6.

Onion Pie

1 cup butter cracker crumbs
¼ cup melted butter
1 quart sliced onions
  (yellow or Walla Walla)

¼ cup chicken broth
  (canned or cube),
  lightly salted
1½ cups milk
4 eggs, slightly beaten
½ cup or more grated cheese

Mix the crumbs and butter; line a 10-inch pie plate. Cook the onions over low heat in the seasoned broth. Pour into the crust. Mix the milk and eggs, and pour over the onions. Sprinkle with the cheese. Bake at 350° for 30 minutes.

Serves 4 to 6.

Toasted Roasted Potatoes

8 medium potatoes
½ cup melted butter
1½ cups fine dry crumbs

1 egg, beaten
Salt & pepper

Peel the potatoes; wash and dry well. Roll the potatoes in ¼ cup melted butter, then in the dry crumbs. Dip in the beaten egg and then roll in crumbs again. Place in a greased casserole. Season with salt and pepper, and drizzle on the remaining ¼ cup melted butter. Bake at 400° for 1 hour.

Serves 8.

Zucchini Pudding

2 pounds small zucchini
1 (4½ ounce) can chopped
   ripe olives
1 cup grated cheddar cheese
3 tablespoons minced onion
1 small clove garlic, minced
   (optional)
2 eggs

½ cup milk
½ teaspoon Worcestershire
   sauce
Dash thyme
Salt & pepper to taste
1 cup fine, soft bread crumbs
1 tablespoon melted butter
Paprika

Wash the zucchini and trim off the ends. Cook whole in boiling, salted water for 15 minutes, or just until tender. Drain, chop coarsely, and drain again. Mix the zucchini, olives, cheese, onion, and garlic. Beat the eggs until light. Blend in the milk, and then add to the zucchini. Season with Worcestershire sauce, thyme, salt, and pepper. Turn the mixture into a greased 10x6x2-inch baking dish. Toss the bread crumbs and melted butter. Sprinkle over the pudding. Dust with paprika. Bake at 350° for 45-50 minutes or until firm in the center.

To reheat leftover pudding, cover the baking dish tightly with aluminum foil, set it in a shallow pan of hot water, and bake at 350° until piping hot.

Serves 6.

Potato Pudding

2 cups finely diced potatoes
1 ½ cups hot milk
4 eggs, slightly beaten
⅓ cup chopped onion

1 ½ teaspoons salt
⅛ teaspoon pepper
1-2 tablespoons chopped
  parsley

Cook the potatoes in 1 cup boiling water until tender; drain. Save the liquid for soups. Stir the milk into the eggs. The milk should not be hot enough to cook the eggs. Add the potatoes, onion, salt, pepper, and chopped parsley. Mix well. Pour into a greased 1 ½ quart casserole. Bake at 350° for 40 minutes or until set.

Serves 4.

Washington Potatoes

6 large potatoes, peeled
  & thinly sliced
1 ½ cups chopped onions
3 cups thinly sliced celery
1 ½ cups beer
1 ½ cups chicken stock
1 ½ teaspoons salt

¼ teaspoon pepper
⅓ cup melted butter
¾ cup dry bread crumbs
⅓ cup grated Parmesan
  cheese or 1 cup grated
  cheddar cheese
1 teaspoon paprika
¼ teaspoon garlic powder

In a 2½ quart casserole, layer the potatoes, onions, and celery. Combine the beer, chicken stock, salt, and pepper. Pour over the vegetables. Cover. Bake at 350° for 1 hour or until potatoes are done. Remove. Combine the melted butter, bread crumbs, Parmesan or cheddar cheese, paprika, and garlic powder. Uncover the casserole and sprinkle with the crumb mixture. Continue to bake, uncovered, for an additional 10 minutes or until golden brown.

Serves 8.

Baked Barbecue Potatoes

1 tablespoon flour
1 ½ teaspoons salt
⅛ teaspoon pepper
4 cups thinly sliced raw
  potatoes
½ cup chopped onion
1 cup shredded cheddar
  cheese

⅓ cup catsup
1 teaspoon Worcestershire
  sauce
3 drops hot pepper sauce
¾ cup canned milk
¾ cup boiling water
2 tablespoons butter
4 slices bacon, diced, fried
  crisp, & drained

Combine the flour, salt, and pepper; mix. Arrange the sliced raw potatoes, chopped onion, flour mixture, and ½ cup cheese in layers in a buttered, shallow 2 quart casserole. Combine the catsup, Worcestershire sauce, hot pepper sauce, canned milk, and boiling water; mix. Pour over the potatoes and dot with the butter. Cover and bake at 375° for 45 minutes. Uncover and stir. Continue baking until the potatoes are tender, 15-20 minutes. Sprinkle with the remaining ½ cup cheese and the diced bacon. Serve at once.

Serves 4 to 6.

Oven-Fried Potato Skins

4 medium baking potatoes
  (about 1 ½ pounds)

4 tablespoons butter
Salt & pepper

Scrub the potatoes thoroughly and pat them dry. Bake the potatoes directly on the center rack of the oven at 450° for about 1 hour, or until tender. Cut the potatoes in half lengthwise and scoop out the insides with a spoon, leaving a shell about ⅛-inch thick; reserve the pulp for another use. Cut each shell lengthwise into ½-inch strips. In a large skillet, melt the butter over low heat. Add the potato skins and toss until well coated. Arrange the strips on a baking sheet, skin side down, and bake for about 15 minutes, or until crisp and golden brown. Sprinkle with salt and pepper to taste. Serve hot or at room temperature.

Serves 2 teenagers.

177

Sweet Potatoes

10 large sweet potatoes or
   2 cans sweet potatoes
1 teaspoon salt
½ teaspoon cinnamon

¾ teaspoon mace
1½ cups brown sugar
1-1½ cups orange or
   pineapple juice
4 tablespoons butter

Peel the sweet potatoes, cut them in half lengthwise, and parboil them, or use canned sweet potatoes. Place the pieces in a flat baking dish. Mix the salt, cinnamon, mace, and brown sugar. Sprinkle over the potatoes. Pour the orange or pineapple juice over the potatoes. Dot with the butter and bake at 350° for 30 minutes.

Serves 8.

Zucchini Casserole

1 pint small curd creamed
   cottage cheese
1½ teaspoons sweet basil
1 teaspoon oregano
1 clove garlic, minced
¾ cup chopped ripe olives
2 tablespoons butter

2 pounds zucchini, sliced
1 medium onion,
   cut in wedges
¼ cup flour
½ teaspoon salt
2 tablespoons grated
   Parmesan cheese
Paprika

Mix the cottage cheese, basil, oregano, garlic, and ½ cup olives. Heat the butter in a skillet and add the zucchini and onion. Cook on high about 5 minutes, or until tender-crisp. Add the flour and salt; mix. Turn half into a 2 quart dish. Spread the cheese mixture on top, then the remaining zucchini. Sprinkle with Parmesan cheese. Bake, uncovered, at 350° for 30 minutes. Garnish with the rest of the olives and sprinkle with paprika.

Serves 6.

Katherine's Favorite Vegetable Casserole

1 pound fresh mushrooms
sliced
½ cup butter
1 onion, grated
½ cup flour
3 cups milk
¾ pound sharp cheese,
grated
Salt & pepper to taste

Tabasco sauce to taste
Soy sauce to taste
1 package frozen lima beans
1 package frozen green beans
1 package frozen artichoke
hearts, or 1 can, drained
1 (8 ounce) can sliced water
chestnuts
French fried onion rings

Sauté the mushrooms in the butter with the grated onion. Blend in the flour. Slowly add the milk and stir until thick. Add the cheese. When the cheese melts, season the sauce with salt, pepper, Tabasco, and soy sauce. Cook the lima beans, green beans, artichoke hearts, and sliced water chestnuts. Drain and layer in a casserole. Pour the sauce over all. Bake at 350° for 20 minutes. Top with French fried onion rings the last 5 minutes.

Variations:
Substitute canned mushrooms (8 ounces) for fresh.
Use soups instead of cream sauce: mushroom, celery, or cream of chicken.
Add small canned onions or substitute them for artichokes.
Add celery cooked slightly with onions.
Omit the cheese for vegetables only.
Top with buttered crumbs instead of onion rings.
When cheese is omitted, use a small amount of Parmesan or combine Parmesan with crumbs for a different topping.

Serves 16.

Italian Fried Tomatoes

3 large green tomatoes
¼ cup grated Parmesan
  cheese
¼ cup cornmeal

1 tablespoon flour
1 teaspoon seasoned salt
1 teaspoon oregano
Olive oil or vegetable oil
1 clove garlic, minced

Cut a thin slice off the top and bottom of the tomatoes and discard. Cut the tomatoes into ½-inch slices. Dip the slices into a mixture of Parmesan cheese, cornmeal, flour, seasoned salt, and oregano. Fry on both sides until nicely browned in oil with the garlic. Keep hot in the oven until ready to serve: 350° for 10 minutes or 250° for 15 minutes.

Serves 4.

Vegetable Medley Casserole

3 tablespoons butter or
  margarine
1 pound mushrooms, sliced
2 cans cream of mushroom
  soup, undiluted
1 cup light cream or canned
  evaporated milk
2 teaspoons ground dill seed
  or dill weed

2 cups cooked green beans
2 cups cooked lima beans,
  fresh or frozen
1 cup canned whole-kernel
  corn
1 cup coarsely grated
  raw carrots
½ cup grated Parmesan
  cheese

Melt the butter or margarine in a skillet over moderate heat. Add the sliced mushrooms and cook until lightly browned. Blend the soup with the cream or evaporated milk and dill seed or dill weed. Fold in the mushrooms, green beans, lima beans, corn, and carrots. Pour into a greased, deep 2½ quart casserole. Sprinkle with the Parmesan cheese. Bake at 350° for 35-40 minutes or until hot and bubbly.

Serves 12.

Salads

Fruit

Apple & Nut Refrigerator Salad

2 envelopes unflavored gelatin
½ cup water
½ cup sugar
1 cup applesauce
1 cup diced, unpeeled
   red apples

¼ cup chopped walnuts
¼ teaspoon almond extract
2 tablespoons mayonnaise
1 cup whipping cream,
   whipped

In a medium saucepan, soften the gelatin in ½ cup water. Add the sugar and bring to a simmer, stirring until the sugar and gelatin have dissolved. Remove from the heat and add the applesauce. Chill until partially set. Add the diced apples, walnuts, almond extract, and mayonnaise. Fold in the whipped cream. Chill until firm.

Serves 6 to 8.

Leavenworth Apple Salad

1 stick cinnamon
1 teaspoon whole cloves
1 teaspoon whole allspice
3 cups water
3 (3 ounce) packages
   orange gelatin

1 cup white table wine
2-3 Washington Golden
   Delicious apples
3 tablespoons lemon juice
Lettuce

Combine the cinnamon, cloves, allspice, and 1 cup water. Simmer, covered, for 5 minutes. Strain, measure, and add water to make 2 cups. Reheat and dissolve the orange gelatin in it. Stir until completely dissolved and let stand a few minutes; then stir in 1 cup cold water and white table wine. While cooling, peel, core and dice the apples to make 2 cups. Stir and add the lemon juice. When the gelatin is slightly thickened, fold in the diced apples and turn into a 2 quart decorative or ring mold. Chill for several hours or preferably overnight. Unmold and garnish with crisp lettuce to serve.

Serves 8 to 10.

Apple-Cranberry Ribbon Salad

1 (8 ounce) package softened
   cream cheese
¼ cup mayonnaise
1 cup whipped cream
½ cup minced celery
½ cup chopped pecans

2 envelopes unflavored gelatin
½ cup water
2 cups cranberry juice
½ cup sugar
3-4 cored and sliced
   unpared apples

Combine the cream cheese, mayonnaise, and whipped cream. Fold in the celery and pecans. Set aside. Sprinkle the gelatin over ½ cup cold water. Heat the cranberry juice to boiling and stir in the sugar and softened gelatin. Stir until dissolved. Pour 1⅓ cups gelatin mixture in the bottom of an 8x12-inch oblong pan (or 8-inch square pan). Chill slightly. Chill the remaining gelatin until syrupy. Core and slice 1 apple. Arrange the slices in the bottom of the pan. Return to the refrigerator until firm. Spread the cream cheese filling over the first layer; chill. Core and dice 2 or 3 more apples to measure 2 cups and combine with the remaining gelatin. Spoon over the cheese layer. Refrigerate 4 hours or overnight. To serve, unmold on a lettuce-lined platter or cut into individual servings.

Serves 10 to 12.

Continental Salad

3 ripe fresh Bartlett pears,*
   peeled & diced
1 cup thinly sliced celery
1 cup shredded cheddar
   cheese

½ cup chopped nuts
½ cup mayonnaise
¼ cup sherry wine
¼ teaspoon salt
Lettuce cups

Combine the pears, celery, cheese, and nuts. Blend the mayonnaise, sherry wine, and salt. Combine with the pear mixture. Serve in lettuce cups.

*If the salad is to stand, stir 1 tablespoon fresh lemon juice or 1 teaspoon Fruit Fresh into the diced pears.

Serves about 6 to 8.

186

Layered Cranberry-Apple-Grapefruit Salad

Cranberry layer:
1 (3 ounce) package
  strawberry flavored gelatin
1 cup boiling water
1 (16 ounce) can whole
  cranberry sauce
1 apple
½ lemon
½ cup diced celery

Apple layer:
1 (3 ounce) package
  lemon flavored gelatin
1¼ cups boiling water
¼ cup lemon juice

1 (8 ounce) package
  cream cheese
1 apple, peeled, cored,
  & diced
½ cup salted cashew nuts,
  chopped

Grapefruit layer:
1 (3 ounce) package
  lime flavored gelatin
1 cup boiling water
1 (8 ounce) can grapefruit
  sections or 1 cup fresh
  grapefruit sections
Bibb lettuce
Grapes, seeded & frosted

Cranberry layer: Dissolve the strawberry flavored gelatin in boiling water. Stir in the can of whole cranberry sauce. Chill until partially set. Peel, halve, and core the apple. Reserve 1 half, rubbing the surface with lemon juice. Cut the remaining apple half in slices; arrange the slices around the bottom of an 8-cup mold. Fold the diced celery into the partially set gelatin; spoon over the apple slices in the mold. Chill until the mixture is almost set.

Apple layer: Meanwhile, dissolve the lemon flavored gelatin in boiling water. Stir in the lemon juice. Gradually add to the cream cheese, softened, beating smooth with a mixer. Chill until partially set. Stir in the diced apple and chopped cashew nuts. Spoon over the cranberry layer. Chill until almost firm.

Grapefruit layer: Meanwhile, dissolve the lime flavored gelatin in boiling water. Drain a can of grapefruit sections, reserving the syrup (or 1 cup fresh grapefruit sections); add water to the syrup to make ¾ cup. Add the syrup to the gelatin, setting the fruit aside. Chill until partially set. Dice the reserved half apple. Fold the apple and grapefruit into the gelatin. Spoon over the lemon layer. Chill until firm, 6 hours or overnight. Garnish with bibb lettuce and seeded frosted grapes.

Serves 12.

187

Mother's Cranberry Salad

1 quart cranberries
1 orange, quartered,
   seeded, & diced with peel
2 cups sugar

2 (3 ounce) packages
   cherry flavored gelatin
2 cups boiling water
4 apples, diced
1 cup crushed pineapple

Wash and drain the cranberries. Grind the raw cranberries and orange. (You can use a blender instead of grinding.) If the orange is heavy skinned, use only part of the peel. Cover with the sugar and let stand until dissolved, about 2 hours. Dissolve the cherry gelatin in boiling water. Stir until dissolved. When cool and beginning to set, add the diced apples, crushed pineapple, and sugared cranberries and orange. Mold in a flat container. Cut as desired and serve on lettuce with salad dressing or whipped cream.

Variation: Use 1 can whole-cranberry sauce instead of fresh cranberries.

Serves 10 to 12.

Heavenly Hash Marlow

¼ pound (16) large
   marshmallows
1 cup crushed pineapple

12 maraschino cherries,
   quartered
½ cup nutmeats, chopped
1 cup whipping cream,
   whipped

Place the marshmallows and 2 tablespoons crushed pineapple in a saucepan. Heat slowly, folding over and over until the marshmallows are half melted. Remove from the heat and continue folding until the mixture is smooth and fluffy. Cool slightly, then blend in the remainder of the pineapple, maraschino cherries, and nutmeats. Fold in the whipped cream. Pour into a tray and freeze without stirring.

Serves 8.

Frozen Fruit Salad

1 (11 ounce) can Mandarin
  orange slices
1 (13½ ounce) can pineapple
  tidbits
1 envelope unflavored gelatin

2 (8 ounce) cartons orange-
  pineapple yogurt
½ cup maraschino
  cherry halves
1 cup flaked coconut
½ pint whipping cream

Thoroughly drain the canned fruits, reserving the syrup. Measure ½ cup syrup and add gelatin to it. Dissolve the gelatin by placing over boiling water. Stir together the gelatin and orange-pineapple yogurt. Add the drained fruits, cherries, and coconut. Whip the whipping cream until stiff. Fold into the gelatin mixture. Spoon into a 9x9-inch baking dish, 2 quart salad mold, or individual molds. Cover with foil and freeze quickly. Move from freezer to refrigerator 1 hour before serving. The gelatin will retain the shape of the salad even if it defrosts.

Other fruits such as bananas, seedless grapes, or fruit cocktail may be substituted for Mandarin oranges and pineapple.

Makes 10 to 12 servings.

189

Purple Plum Salad

½ cup granulated sugar
¾ cup water
1 (3 ounce) package
   lemon flavored gelatin
½ cup orange juice
1 teaspoon orange peel

1 ½ cups coarsely cut fresh
   prune plums, or other
   plums in season
1 cup seeded white grape
   halves, or green grapes
½ cup chopped nuts
Crisp greens

Stir the sugar and water together in a medium size saucepan; continue stirring over medium-high heat until the mixture comes to a boil. Dissolve the lemon gelatin in the hot syrup. Add the orange juice and orange peel. Chill until partially set. Fold in the cut plums, grapes, and nuts. Turn into a 1 ½ quart oiled mold and chill until firm. To serve: unmold onto a serving dish. Garnish with crisp greens.

Serve with mayonnaise to which has been added a little orange juice and orange peel.

Serves 6.

Strawberry Ambrosia Salad

1 (3 ounce) package
   strawberry gelatin
1 (3 ounce) package
   raspberry gelatin
2 cups boiling water
1 (10 ounce) package
   frozen, sweetened,
   & sliced strawberries

½ cup cold water
1 (8¼ ounce) can crushed
   pineapple with syrup
⅓ cup flaked coconut
⅔ cup evaporated milk
Lettuce

Dissolve the strawberry and raspberry gelatins in boiling water in a medium bowl. Place the frozen strawberries in the dissolved gelatin. Break up the strawberries with a fork; stir until thawed. Stir in the cold water and pineapple. Chill until it is the consistency of unbeaten egg whites. Add the coconut and evaporated milk. Mix well. Pour into a 5-cup mold. Chill at least 4 hours. Unmold on lettuce leaves.

Serves 6 to 8.

Vegetable

Rudy Vallee Salad

1 head iceberg lettuce,
  cut into cubes
2 tomatoes, peeled & cut
  into eighths

1 cucumber, halved & sliced
½ cup chopped parsley
Salt & pepper
⅓ cup oil
⅓ cup vinegar

Mix the cut vegetables lightly in a bowl. Add the salt, pepper, oil, and vinegar. Toss to mix and serve in attractive individual bowls or on salad plates.

Serves 4 to 6.

Corn Salad

Dressing:
⅓ cup vegetable oil
2 tablespoons lemon juice
1 tablespoon vinegar
1 clove garlic,
  peeled & minced
¼ teaspoon salt
⅛ teaspoon pepper
½ teaspoon sugar
1 teaspoon dried parsley
  flakes or 1 tablespoon
  chopped fresh parsley

1 tablespoon chopped sweet
  pickles or 1 tablespoon
  pickle relish

1 (12 ounce) can golden
  whole-kernel corn, drained
½ teaspoon salt
2 pimentos, chopped
4 slices red or yellow onion,
  separated
Romaine
Bacon chips

Dressing: Measure the vegetable oil into a 1 cup measuring cup and add the lemon juice, vinegar, garlic, salt, pepper, sugar, parsley, and sweet pickles. Mix well.

In a small bowl, place the corn, salt, pimentos, and onions. Toss gently to mix. Add the oil and vinegar dressing to the corn mixture and toss gently to coat. This salad can be served at once or chilled in a refrigerator. Serve with crisp, sliced romaine and sprinkle with bacon chips.

Serves 4.

Cabbage-Pineapple Slaw

3 cups thinly shredded
   crisp cabbage
1 cup fresh pineapple chunks
1 cup diced apples
1 cup marshmallows (10),
   cut into eighths

½ cup chopped celery
½ cup mayonnaise
Red apple wedges
Avocados
Lemon juice

Combine the shredded cabbage, pineapple chunks, diced apples, marshmallows, and celery. Add the mayonnaise, and toss until all ingredients are coated. Garnish with the red apple wedges and avocados dipped in lemon juice.

Serves 6.

Cobb Salad

½ head lettuce, finely chopped
½ bunch watercress,
   finely chopped
1 small bunch chicory
   (optional)
½ head romaine,
   finely chopped
2 medium-size tomatoes,
   peeled
2 breasts of boiled
   roasting chicken

6 strips crisp bacon
1 avocado
3 hard-boiled eggs, chopped
2 tablespoons chopped chives
½ cup finely chopped
   imported Roquefort cheese
1 cup **Brown Derby Old-
   Fashioned French Dressing**
   (see index)

Combine the lettuce, watercress, chicory, and romaine in a salad bowl. Cut the tomatoes in half, remove the seeds, dice finely, and arrange in a strip across the salad. Dice the breasts of chicken and arrange over the top of the chopped greens. Chop the bacon finely and sprinkle over the salad. Cut the avocado in small pieces and arrange around the edge of the salad. Decorate the salad by sprinkling the chopped eggs, chives, and cheese over the top. Just before serving, mix the salad thoroughly with **Brown Derby Old-Fashioned French Dressing.**

Serves 4 to 6.

194

Day Before-Vegetable Salad

Herb Marinade:
1½ cups corn oil
½ cup red wine vinegar
3 tablespoons light corn syrup
2 teaspoons salt
1 teaspoon basil leaves
½ teaspoon seasoned pepper

1½ cups sliced fresh
  mushrooms
1 (1 pound) can green beans,
  drained
1 (1 pound) can garbanzo
  beans, drained

1 (1 pound) lima beans,
  drained
1 (1 pound) can asparagus
  spears, drained
Lettuce
Olives
Cucumbers, sliced
Green onions, sliced
Cherry tomatoes
1 cup mayonnaise
¼ cup chopped green pepper
¼ cup chopped pimento
1 tablespoon minced
  green onion
1 tablespoon chopped parsley

Herb Marinade: Place the corn oil, red wine vinegar, light corn syrup, salt, basil leaves, and seasoned pepper in a 1 quart jar. Cover; shake to blend.

Combine the mushrooms in a bowl with the green beans, garbanzo beans, lima beans, and asparagus spears (or vegetables of your choice). Cover with the **Herb Marinade.** Marinate overnight in the refrigerator. When ready to serve, drain the marinade and reserve. Line a tray, large platter, or bowl with lettuce leaves. Add lettuce chunks, olives, cucumbers, and green onions to the salad. Mound the vegetables on the lettuce. Garnish with the cherry tomatoes. Serve with creamy vegetable dressing made by combining ½ cup reserved **Herb Marinade**, mayonnaise, green pepper, pimento, green onion, and parsley.

This is an excellent recipe to take on a boat.

Serves 10 to 12.

Del Mar Molded Salad

2-3 avocados (2 cups sieved)
3 tablespoons lemon juice
1¾ teaspoons salt
⅛ teaspoon Tabasco
1½ envelopes unflavored
    gelatin (1½ tablespoons)
½ cup cold water

1 cup boiling water
1 cup dairy sour cream
1 cup mayonnaise
¼ cup sliced green onions
1 large tomato, peeled,
    seeded, & diced
Salad greens

Cut the avocados in half; peel, mash, and sieve, or whiz in the blender until smooth. Blend in the lemon juice, salt, and Tabasco. Soften the gelatin in cold water; dissolve in 1 cup boiling water; cool to room temperature. Stir in the seasoned avocado, sour cream, and mayonnaise; chill until the mixture mounds on a spoon. Fold in the onion and tomato and turn into 5-cup ring mold. Chill until firm. Unmold and garnish with salad greens.

Serves 6 to 8.

Overnight Salad

1 head iceberg lettuce
1 bunch spinach
½ cup thinly sliced
    green onions
1 cup thinly sliced celery
1 (8 ounce) can water
    chestnuts, drained & sliced
1 package frozen green peas
2 cups mayonnaise

2 tablespoons sugar
½ cup grated Parmesan
    cheese
1 teaspoon seasoned salt
¼ teaspoon garlic powder
3 hard-boiled eggs, chopped
½-¾ pound bacon, crisply
    fried & crumbled
2 tomatoes, cut into wedges

Shred the lettuce and spinach and combine them in the bottom of a bowl. Top with green onions, celery, water chestnuts, and green peas. Spread the mayonnaise evenly over the top and sprinkle with sugar, Parmesan, salt, and garlic powder. Cover and chill up to 24 hours. Just before serving, sprinkle with eggs and crumbled bacon. Arrange tomatoes around the edge.

Serve with French bread or whole wheat wafers and fresh fruit for dessert.

Fresh Mushroom Salad

1 pound mushrooms
3 chopped green onions
4 teaspoons lemon juice
1 teaspoon Worcestershire
  sauce

½ teaspoon dry mustard
⅔ cup oil
½ teaspoon salt
⅛ teaspoon pepper
12 slices bacon

Rinse and pat dry the mushrooms. Mix together the green onions, lemon juice, Worcestershire sauce, dry mustard, oil, salt, and pepper. Marinate the mushrooms in the mixture for at least 4 hours. Fry the bacon crisp. Crumble it over the top of the mushrooms just before serving. Serve on a lettuce cup.

This recipe comes from the University of Washington Alumnae Club's Holiday Fair.

Summer Platter

¼ cup salad oil
⅓ cup wine vinegar
¼ cup lemon juice
¼ cup water
1 cup chopped celery
1 tablespoon capers
1 teaspoon Italian seasoning

½ teaspoon salt
Freshly ground pepper
1 (8½ ounce) can small
  artichoke hearts
2 medium tomatoes, sliced
1 (8 ounce) package elbow
  macaroni

Combine the salad oil, vinegar, lemon juice, water, celery, capers, Italian seasoning, salt, and pepper. Pour over the artichokes and tomatoes; allow to marinate several hours in the refrigerator. Add 1 tablespoon salt to 3 quarts rapidly boiling water. Gradually add the macaroni so that water continues to boil. Cook uncovered, stirring occasionally, until tender. Drain in a colander. Remove the artichokes and tomatoes from the marinade, and arrange around the edge of a platter. Toss the macaroni with the marinade and place in the center of the platter.

Each serving is about 190 calories.

Serves 8.

Baked Potato Salad

3 medium onions, sliced
3 tablespoons butter
6 hard-boiled eggs
6 potatoes, cooked,
    peeled, & sliced

Salt & pepper
1 cup sour cream
2 tablespoons butter, melted
½ cup bread crumbs

Sauté the sliced onions in butter. Slice the eggs. Layer the potatoes, eggs, and onions in a buttered casserole beginning and ending with potatoes. Season each layer of ingredients with salt and pepper and spread with the sour cream. Combine the melted butter and bread crumbs. Sprinkle the top of the casserole with the crumbs and bake at 350° for 45 minutes.

Serves 6.

Summer Rice Salad

1 (13¾ ounce) can
    chicken broth
1 cup rice or bulgur wheat
1 tablespoon olive oil
    or vegetable oil
3 tablespoons wine vinegar
½ teaspoon dried dillweed or
    1 tablespoon snipped fresh
    dillweed

½ teaspoon dried sweet
    basil leaves
½ teaspoon salt
¼ teaspoon pepper
1 cup halved cherry tomatoes
1 cup sliced celery
1 cup thinly sliced,
    peeled carrots

In a heavy 2 quart saucepan, bring the chicken broth to a boil over moderately high heat. Add the rice or bulgur wheat. Return to a boil, and then reduce the heat to low. Cover the pan, and cook 20 minutes or until rice or bulgur is tender and the broth has been absorbed. Tip the rice into a salad bowl. Add the oil, wine vinegar, dillweed, basil, salt, and pepper, and toss gently to mix. Cover and refrigerate 2 hours, or longer, to chill and blend the flavors. Just before serving, add the tomatoes, celery, and carrots and toss.

Serves 4.

Spirit of '76 Picnic Salad

1 head iceberg lettuce
2 medium-size tomatoes
1 green pepper
8-10 radishes
2-3 green onions
1 teaspoon sugar
½ teaspoon seasoned salt

½ teaspoon dry mustard
½ teaspoon paprika
½ teaspoon chili powder
2 tablespoons lemon juice
2 tablespoons vinegar
½ cup corn oil

Core, rinse, and drain the head of lettuce thoroughly. Wash the tomatoes, green pepper, radishes, and green onions. Trim the radishes and onions. Place the lettuce along with the other vegetables in a plastic bowl with a cover or in a plastic bag. Chill. Combine the sugar, seasoned salt, dry mustard, paprika, and chili powder in a small plastic bowl or a jar with a cover. Stir in the lemon juice and vinegar. Add the corn oil, cover, and shake to blend. Carry the plastic containers to the picnic. Just before serving, tear the lettuce in bite-size pieces, cut the tomatoes into wedges, the green pepper into strips, and slice the radishes and onions. Combine. Shake the dressing to blend and pour over the vegetables. Toss lightly.

Serves 6.

Western Way Salad

Croutons:
2 cups cubed (⅓-inch) bread
1 clove garlic
¼ cup olive oil

3 quarts salad greens,
    such as romaine & lettuce,
    washed, drained, & chilled
½ cup salad oil
1 tablespoon Worcestershire
    sauce

Black pepper, freshly ground
Salt
¼ cup grated Parmesan
    cheese
¼ cup crumbled Roquefort-
    type cheese
1 raw egg
2-3 medium lemons,
    cut in half, seeded
4-5 anchovy fillets,
    cut in pieces (optional)

Croutons: Toast the bread cubes to a golden brown in a very slow oven. The cubes must be very crisp and dry throughout. Cut the garlic into the olive oil and let stand to extract flavor. Pour the garlic-flavored oil over the crisp bread cubes, holding back the bits of garlic. Saturate the cubes thoroughly with the oil just before adding to the salad.

Break or cut the salad greens into generous bite-size pieces. Place them in a very large bowl and add the remaining ingredients. Be spectacular! Drop the uncooked, unbeaten egg onto the greens! If you wish, first coddle the egg for 1 minute in boiling water. With a fork ream out the lemon juice directly onto the salad. Toss the salad well. At the very last moment, add the **Croutons** to the salad. Toss again lightly. Serve at once while croutons are crisp. Garnish with anchovies, if desired.

This is an interesting salad to prepare at the dining table for a first course. (Ask a guest with gourmet tendencies to preside at the ceremony!) The egg, broken onto the greens, catches the cheese and blends it with the oil into a smooth, flavorful coating for each salad leaf. The lemon juice adds a just-right tartness. The croutons give a pleasing texture contrast. The directions look complicated but are not. Just assemble the ingredients, mix as directed, and serve at once.

Serves 8 to 10.

Spinach Salad

Salad Dressing:
1 egg
1 ½ tablespoons sugar
½ teaspoon salt
¼ teaspoon paprika
½ teaspoon dry mustard
¼ cup catsup
1 cup salad oil

¼ cup vinegar
¼ cup warm water

2 bunches spinach
6 strips bacon
1 clove garlic
1 tablespoon lemon juice

Salad Dressing: Place in blender the egg, sugar, salt, paprika, and dry mustard. Blend and add the catsup, salad oil, and vinegar. Blend again and add warm water. Blend.

Wash the spinach, remove the stems, and drain well. Break it into bite-size pieces. Refrigerate. Cut strips of bacon into small pieces and fry until crisp. Drain the bacon. Reserve 1 tablespoon bacon fat. Now rub the garlic clove in a wooden salad bowl, add the spinach leaves, and moisten the leaves with some reserved bacon fat and the lemon juice. Add the crisp bacon. Toss. Place in individual salad bowls, on a lettuce leaf if you wish, and pour some of the **Salad Dressing** over each salad.

This dressing is excellent with all green salads and fruit salads, too.

Serve 4 to 6.

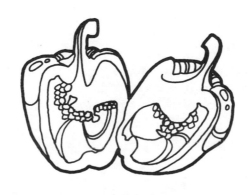

Dressings

Brown Derby Old-Fashioned French Dressing

1 cup water
1 cup red wine vinegar
1 teaspoon sugar
Juice of ½ lemon
2½ tablespoons salt
1 tablespoon freshly
    ground black pepper

1 tablespoon Worcestershire
    sauce
1 teaspoon dry mustard
1 bud garlic, chopped
1 cup olive oil
3 cups salad oil

Blend together all ingredients except the oils. Then add the olive and salad oils and mix well again. Chill. Shake before serving.

Blender Green Goddess Dressing

1 egg
4 tablespoons white
    wine vinegar
1 tablespoon lemon juice
1 teaspoon sugar
1 teaspoon French mustard
1 cup salad oil

1 (2 ounce) can anchovies,
    chopped
1 tablespoon tarragon
1 teaspoon garlic salt
1 green onion, chopped
1 cup minced parsley
1 cup sour cream

Place in a blender the egg, 2 tablespoons vinegar, lemon juice, sugar and mustard. Cover and blend a few seconds. Remove the cap, and with the motor running, slowly pour in the salad oil in a steady stream, blending until smooth. Add the chopped anchovies, tarragon, and garlic salt. Blend. Add the chopped green onion and minced parsley. Blend until finely minced. Add the remaining 2 tablespoons vinegar and the sour cream, and blend a few seconds.

Makes 3 cups.

"Specialty of the House" Salad Dressing

1 cup mayonnaise
¼ cup olive oil
2 tablespoons tarragon
  white wine vinegar
1 tablespoon Dijon mustard
⅛ teaspoon crushed
  tarragon leaves

⅛ teaspoon crushed
  oregano leaves
¼ teaspoon white pepper
¼ teaspoon salt
¼ cup fresh, chopped parsley
2 hard-boiled eggs,
  sliced & diced

Combine all ingredients and mix thoroughly. Store in the refrigerator. This dressing is excellent with greens, vegetables, and fish and meat salads.

Makes 2 cups.

Creamy Dill Dressing

1 (8 ounce) carton
  cottage cheese
¼ cup milk
2 tablespoons salad oil

1¼ teaspoons crushed
  dill weed
¼ teaspoon salt
⅛ teaspoon pepper

Place all ingredients in a blender; cover. Blend on high speed until smooth. Refrigerate covered at least 3 hours to allow flavors to mellow. Serve over tossed green salad.

Approximately 20 calories per tablespoon.

Makes 1½ cups dressing.

Pineapple Fruit Salad Dressing

1 tablespoon cornstarch
½ cup sugar
2 egg yolks, slightly beaten
1 tablespoon grated
   lemon peel

⅓ cup water
3 tablespoons pineapple
   juice
2 tablespoons lemon juice
⅛ teaspoon salt

Mix the cornstarch and sugar together. Add the egg yolks, lemon peel, and water. Cook over direct heat, bringing the mixture to a boil. Boil 1 minute stirring constantly. Remove from heat; add the pineapple juice, lemon juice, and salt. Cool. Pour over a scoop of ice cream and frozen mixed fruit.

Serves 6.

Honey Dressing

½ cup salad oil
¼ cup lemon juice
½ teaspoon paprika

2 tablespoons honey
¼ teaspoon salt
2 ripe mashed bananas

Combine all ingredients and mix until thoroughly blended. Chill. Shake well before serving.

This dressing is excellent for fruit salads.

Makes 1 ⅓ cups.

Eggs

Carol's Egg Casserole

8 slices white bread,
  crusts removed
¾ pound sharp cheddar
  cheese, grated
1 cup sautéed mushrooms
2 pounds crab or browned
  pork link sausage

4 eggs
¾ teaspoon dry mustard
2¼ cups milk
1 can mushroom soup,
  undiluted
⅓ cup milk

The night before, layer the bread, cheese, mushrooms, and crab or sausage in 9x13-inch or 11x15-inch dish. Mix the eggs, mustard, and milk, and pour over the layered ingredients. Refrigerate. Just before serving, mix the soup and ⅓ cup milk. Pour over the casserole. Bake at 325° for 1¾ hours.

Serve with fresh strawberries and pineapple or fruit in season. Carol has used this recipe with salmon and also with ground beef replacing the crab.

Cheese Fondue

2 cups milk
2 cups grated sharp
  cheddar cheese
1 tablespoon butter
1 teaspoon salt

Dash pepper
3 eggs, separated
  (at room temperature)
4 slices white bread, toasted
  & cut into ¼-inch cubes

Heat all the ingredients except the eggs and bread until the milk is scalded. Beat the egg yolks until thick and lemon-colored. Slowly stir the hot milk mixture into the beaten yolks. Beat the egg whites until stiff; fold into the hot mixture. Pour into an ungreased baking dish, 8x8x2-inches or 6x10x2-inches. Sprinkle with bread cubes in an even layer. Set in a pan of hot water (1-inch deep). Bake at 350° for 45 minutes or until a knife inserted in the center comes out clean.

Serves 4 to 6.

Cheese Soufflé

4 tablespoons butter
4 tablespoons flour
1½ cups milk
½ teaspoon salt

¼ teaspoon dry mustard
½ pound sharp cheddar
   cheese, cubed
6 eggs, separated
   (at room temperature)

Melt the butter in a saucepan. Blend in the flour. Add the milk very slowly, stirring constantly to make a smooth white sauce. Allow to cook about 5 minutes or until no starchy taste remains. Remove from the heat and add the salt, dry mustard, and cheese. Stir until the cheese is all melted. Beat the egg yolks and stir into the sauce; allow to cool to room temperature. Beat the egg whites until stiff. Fold into the sauce and pour the mixture into a 2 quart baking dish. Bake at 300° for about 1¼ hours or until puffy and brown.

Serves 6.

Easy Cheese Puff

8 slices bread, crusts removed
½ cup chopped onion
½ cup chopped celery
1 tablespoon butter or
   margarine
¼ cup chopped green
   chiles (optional)

8 slices American cheese
3 eggs
2 cups milk
½ teaspoon seasoned salt
⅛ teaspoon pepper
½ teaspoon paprika

Fit 4 slices of bread into the bottom of a square glass baking dish or cake pan. Sauté the onion and celery in butter or margarine until limp; sprinkle over the bread in the dish. If using green chiles, scatter over the mixture. Place 2 slices of cheese on each slice of bread. Cover with the remaining bread. Beat the eggs; add the milk, salt, pepper, and paprika, mixing well. Pour over the bread in the casserole. Cover and store in the refrigerator for at least 1 hour. Bake at 350° for 1 hour, or until puffed and golden brown. Serve immediately.

Serves 4.

Eggs Fantastic

1 pound ground sausage
½ pound fresh mushrooms,
  chopped
1 medium onion, diced
Salt & pepper
6 eggs, blended
3 tablespoons sour cream

5 ounces Mexican tomato &
  green chile hot sauce
8 ounces medium cheddar
  cheese, grated
8 ounces mozzarella cheese,
  grated
8 ounces Velveeta cheese,
  grated

Sauté the sausage, mushrooms, and onion; add salt and pepper to taste. Drain and set aside. Combine the eggs and sour cream in a blender and whip 1 minute. Grease a baking pan, 9x13x2-inch, and add the blended eggs. Place in a 400° oven until the eggs are set (a few minutes). Remove from the oven, and spoon the hot sauce over; add the sausage, mushrooms, and onion mixture. Top with 3 layers of cheese. Put under the broiler until the cheese melts. Bake 45 minutes at 350°.

This recipe may be prepared the night before and baked in the morning. Tomato sauce may be used instead of hot sauce.

The Impossible Quiche

3 eggs
½ cup biscuit mix
½ cup melted butter
1 ½ cups milk
¼ teaspoon salt

Dash pepper
1 cup shredded Swiss cheese
½ cup diced ham or bacon,
  cooked & cut into
  small pieces

Mix all the ingredients except the cheese and ham or bacon with a rotary beater. Pour the mixture into a greased 9-inch pie pan. Sprinkle cheese and meat over the top, and press below the surface of the egg mixture with the back of a spoon. Bake at 350° for 45 minutes. Allow to set 10 minutes before cutting.

Serves 4 to 6.

John Wayne Soufflé

2 (4 ounce) cans green
   chiles, drained, diced,
   & seeds removed
1 pound Monterey Jack
   cheese, coarsely grated
1 pound cheddar cheese,
   coarsely grated

4 eggs, separated
2/3 cup evaporated milk
1 tablespoon flour
1/2 teaspoon salt
1/8 teaspoon pepper
2 medium tomatoes, sliced

In a large bowl, combine the chiles and grated cheeses. Turn into a
well-buttered 2 quart casserole, about 12x8x2-inches. In a large mixer
bowl, beat the egg whites with an electric mixer at high speed until stiff
peaks are formed. In small mixer, combine the egg yolks, milk, flour,
salt, and pepper. Mix until well blended. With a rubber scraper, gently
fold the beaten egg whites into the yolk mixture, then pour over the
cheese mixture in the casserole, using a fork to "ooze" through the
cheese; don't whip it. Bake at 325° for 30 minutes. Arrange sliced
tomatoes around the edge of casserole and bake 30 minutes longer. If
desired, garnish with more chiles.

This recipe comes from Paul Harvey.

Serves 6 to 8.

Larry's Sunrise Soufflé

1 slice whole wheat bread
Butter
1 large egg

1 tablespoon milk
2 tablespoons diced
   cream cheese
Dash salt

Roll the bread thin with a rolling pin. Lightly butter each side of the
bread. Place it in a buttered 6-inch Pyrex dish. Whip the egg lightly with
milk. Pour over the bread and add diced chunks of cream cheese. Add
a dash of salt. Place in the microwave oven on *HIGH* for 1-1½ minutes.
When the cheese melts and soufflé is puffed, serve immediately.

Serves 1.

Katherine's Quick Quiche

1 cup Italian-style
   bread crumbs
6 slices bacon
1 large onion, finely chopped
½ cup grated Swiss cheese

4 eggs, slightly beaten
1 cup milk
1 cup evaporated milk
Pinch nutmeg
½ teaspoon salt
¼ teaspoon pepper

Butter a 9-inch pie plate. Spread the bread crumbs evenly over the bottom and about ½-inch up the sides of the pie plate. In a heavy skillet, fry the bacon until crisp. Remove the bacon and set aside. Add the onion to the bacon fat and fry until clear. While the onion is cooking, crumble the cooled bacon over the crumbs. When the onion is cooked, tilt to drain, and spoon the onion with a slotted spoon over the bacon. Cover with the grated Swiss cheese. In a mixing bowl, combine the eggs, milk, evaporated milk, nutmeg, salt, and pepper. Mix well. Ladle carefully over the bacon mixture. Bake at 350° for 30 minutes or until the custard is set and golden.

Serves 4 to 6.

Quiche Lorraine

8 slices bacon
¼ cup chopped onion
¾ cup grated Swiss cheese
1 (9-inch) unbaked pie shell
3 eggs

½ teaspoon salt
⅛ teaspoon pepper
Dash cayenne pepper
1½ cups half & half or
   evaporated milk
Nutmeg

Fry the bacon until crisp, reserving fat. Crumble into bits. Sauté onion in 1½ tablespoons bacon fat. Sprinkle the bacon and grated Swiss cheese onto the crust in a 9-inch unbaked pie shell. Add the onions. Beat the eggs until foamy. Add the salt, pepper, cayenne pepper, and half & half. Beat just long enough to mix thoroughly. Pour the cream mixture into the pie crust. Sprinkle lightly with the ground nutmeg, if desired. Bake at 400° for 5 minutes. Reduce the heat to 300° and bake 35-40 minutes more or until done.

Serves 6 to 8.

Breads

Quick Breads

Best Ever Banana Bread

1 cup shortening
2 cups granulated sugar
4 eggs
5 large bananas, mashed
  (2 cups)

3 ½ cups flour
2 teaspoons soda
1 teaspoon salt
1 cup broken walnut meats

Cream the shortening thoroughly. Gradually add the sugar; beat until fluffy. Add the eggs one at a time; beat well after each addition. Beat the bananas to a liquid in a separate bowl. Combine the flour (spooned into a measure and leveled), soda, and salt. Stir the creamed banana mixture and dry ingredients alternately into shortening mixture. Do not beat. Stir in the nuts. Bake in 2 well-greased loaf pans, 9x5x3-inches, at 300° for 1¼ hours, or until firm to the touch.

Makes 2 loaves.

Sunday Morning Coffee Cake

2 cups sifted flour
1 teaspoon baking powder
1 teaspoon soda
1 ½ teaspoons cinnamon
½ teaspoon salt
⅔ cup butter or margarine

1 cup sugar
1 cup brown sugar,
  firmly packed
2 eggs
1 cup buttermilk
½ cup chopped nuts
½ teaspoon nutmeg

Sift together the flour, baking powder, soda, 1 teaspoon cinnamon, and salt. Cream together the butter or margarine, sugar, and ½ cup brown sugar until light and fluffy. Add the eggs, one at a time, beating well after each addition. Add the dry ingredients alternately with the buttermilk, beating well after each addition. Spread the batter into a greased and floured 13x9x2-inch baking pan. Combine ½ cup brown sugar, the chopped nuts, ½ teaspoon cinnamon, and the nutmeg. Mix well. Sprinkle over the batter. Refrigerate 8 hours or overnight. Bake at 350° for 45 minutes or until done. Cut into squares, and serve warm.

Makes 16 servings.

217

Zucchini Bread

1 cup oil
2 cups granulated sugar
3 eggs
3 cups unsifted flour
1 teaspoon salt
1 teaspoon soda

1 teaspoon cinnamon
1 teaspoon nutmeg
1 teaspoon pumpkin pie spice*
½ teaspoon baking powder
2 cups grated zucchini
½ cup chopped nuts
3 teaspoons vanilla

Combine the oil and sugar. Add the eggs, beating well after each addition. Sift together the flour, salt, soda, cinnamon, nutmeg, pumpkin pie spice, and baking powder. Add the zucchini and dry ingredients alternately to the creamed mixture. Blend in the nuts and vanilla. Pour into 2 greased and floured 8½x4½x 2½-inch pans. Bake at 325° for 1 hour.

*¼ teaspoon each of ginger, allspice, mace, and cloves may be substituted for pumpkin pie spice.

Makes 2 medium loaves.

Pumpkin Bread

3 cups sugar
1 cup salad oil
4 eggs, well beaten
2 cups pumpkin
3½ cups sifted flour
2 teaspoons soda
2 teaspoons salt

1 teaspoon baking powder
1 teaspoon nutmeg
1 teaspoon allspice
1 teaspoon cinnamon
½ teaspoon cloves
⅔ cup water
½ cup nutmeats

Cream the sugar and salad oil. Add the eggs and pumpkin, mixing well. Sift the dry ingredients together and then add alternately with the water to the creamed mixture. Add the nuts. Pour into 2 well greased and floured 9x5-inch loaf pans or a 9-cup mini-bundt pan. Bake at 350° for 1-1½ hours or until breads test done. Let stand 10 minutes. Remove from the pans to cool.

Makes 2 loaves.

218

Ready-Bake Bran Muffins

3 cups whole bran cereal
1 cup boiling water
2 eggs, slightly beaten
2 cups buttermilk
½ cup salad oil

1 cup raisins
2½ cups flour
1 cup sugar
½ teaspoon salt
2½ teaspoons soda

In a large bowl, mix the bran cereal and boiling water, stirring to moisten evenly. Set aside until cool, then add the eggs, buttermilk, oil, and raisins; blend well. Stir together the dry ingredients, and add to bran mixture. Spoon the batter into buttered muffin cups, filling ⅔ to ¾ full. Bake at 425° for 20 minutes or until done. This mix keeps for 2-3 weeks in the refrigerator. You can make 2 or 3 muffins at a time, filling empty muffin cups half full with water to prevent the muffins from burning.

These are excellent!

Makes 2½ dozen.

Carol's Triple Rich Wheat Rolls

3 cups warm water
2 cakes yeast
2 tablespoons honey
3 tablespoons wheat germ
½ cup soy flour

¾ cup skim milk powder
4 teaspoons salt
3½ cups whole wheat flour
2 tablespoons salad oil
3½ cups white flour,
    or more, sifted

Combine the water, yeast, and honey. Let this mixture stand for 5 minutes. Combine the wheat germ, soy flour, and skim milk powder, then stir into the yeast mixture along with the salt and all of the whole wheat flour. Add the oil and 3 cups of the white flour. Beat, adding more white flour as needed to make a stiff dough. Knead thoroughly (5 minutes) until smooth and elastic. Place in a greased bowl; turn the dough over. Let rise for 1½ hours. Punch down; let rise another 20 minutes. Shape into 10 large or 20 small rolls. Set side-by-side on a greased pan. Let rise ½ hour. Bake at 350° for 30 minutes.

Swedish Batter Bread

1 package active dry yeast
1¼ cups warm water
2 tablespoons honey or
  brown sugar
2 tablespoons vegetable oil

1 tablespoon caraway seeds,
  optional
2 teaspoons salt
1 cup rye flour
2¾ cups unsifted
  all-purpose flour

In large mixing bowl, sprinkle the yeast over the warm water (105°-115°). Stir until dissolved. Add the honey or brown sugar, vegetable oil, caraway seeds, salt, and rye flour. Beat two minutes. Add the all-purpose flour, and beat until smooth. Cover and let rise in a warm place until doubled, about 30 minutes. Stir down, and then beat 25 strokes. Turn into an oiled 9x5x3-inch loaf pan. Loosely cover and allow to rise in a warm place until the batter reaches the top of the pan, about 40 minutes. Bake at 375° for 45-50 minutes.

Makes 1 loaf.

Martha's Buttermilk Rolls

1 package active dry yeast
¼ cup warm water
¾ cup thick, lukewarm
  buttermilk
1 teaspoon sugar

¼ teaspoon soda
1 teaspoon salt
3 tablespoons soft shortening
2½ cups sifted all-purpose
  flour

Dissolve the yeast in warm water in a mixing bowl. Add the buttermilk, sugar, soda, salt, and shortening. Add half of the sifted flour and mix. Add the remaining flour, and mix in with hands. Knead on a lightly floured board until smooth and elastic. Mold into cloverleaf rolls by forming bits of dough into balls about 1 inch in diameter. Place 3 balls in each of 18 greased muffin pans. Cover with a damp cloth and let rise until double in bulk in a warm place. Bake at 400° for 15-20 minutes.

Makes 18.

English Muffin Bread for Microwave

5 cups flour
2 packages active dry yeast
1 tablespoon sugar
2 teaspoons salt

2½ cups milk
¼ teaspoon soda
1 tablespoon warm water

In a large mixing bowl, combine 3 cups of flour, dry yeast, sugar, and salt. Heat the milk in a saucepan until warm (110°-115°) and add to the flour mixture. Beat until smooth. Stir in enough of 2 cups of flour to make a stiff batter. Cover the bowl, set in a warm place, let rise until doubled in bulk, about 1 hour. Stir down the batter, and thoroughly blend in the soda dissolved in warm water. Divide the batter in two oiled Pyrex dishes, 8½x4½x 2½. Cover and let rise in a warm place until doubled in bulk, about 45 minutes. Cook each loaf separately, uncovered, in the microwave for 6 minutes and 30 seconds, or until no doughy spots remain. Cool for 5 minutes. Loosen the edges and remove from the dish. Cool completely. To serve, slice and toast.

This recipe was developed for use in microwave ovens. It will not brown, but it makes wonderful toast with excellent flavor. This is very close to the original English muffin.

Makes 2 loaves.

Beer Bread

3 cups self-rising flour
3 tablespoons sugar

1 (12 ounce) can beer

Mix all ingredients well. Pour into a greased 9x5x3-inch loaf pan. Brush the top with oil. Bake at 350° for 1 hour.

Variation: For beer bread with herbs, add ¼ teaspoon dry mustard, ½ teaspoon sage and ½ teaspoon celery salt.

Makes 1 loaf.

Cranberry Nut Bread

2 cups all-purpose sifted
   flour
1 cup sugar
1 ½ teaspoons baking powder
½ teaspoon soda
1 teaspoon salt
¼ cup shortening

¾ cup orange juice
1 tablespoon grated
   orange rind
1 egg, well-beaten
½ cup chopped walnuts
1 cup fresh cranberries,
   coarsely chopped

Sift together the flour, sugar, baking powder, soda, and salt. Cut in the shortening until the mixture resembles coarse cornmeal. Combine the orange juice and grated rind with the well-beaten egg. Pour all at once into the dry ingredients, mixing just enough to dampen. Carefully fold in the chopped nuts and cranberries. Spoon into a greased loaf pan, 9x5x3-inch. Spread the corners and sides slightly higher than the center. Bake at 350° for about 1 hour, or until the crust is golden brown and a toothpick inserted comes out clean. Remove from the pan and let cool. Store overnight for easy slicing.

Serves 8 to 10.

Applesauce Nut Bread

2 cups flour
¾ cup sugar
1 teaspoon salt
½ teaspoon soda
½ teaspoon cinnamon

3 teaspoons baking powder
1 cup broken walnuts
1 egg, beaten
2 cups canned applesauce
2 tablespoons shortening,
   melted

Sift the flour, sugar, salt, soda, cinnamon, and baking powder. Add the walnuts. Combine the egg, applesauce, and melted shortening. Add the dry ingredients and stir until just blended. Pour into a greased 9x5x3-inch loaf pan. Bake at 350° for 1 hour or until done.

Serve 8 to 10.

Easy Hot Cross Buns

1 package active dry yeast
1 cup very warm water
 (110°-115°)
2 tablespoons sugar
2¼ cups flour
1 teaspoon salt
1 teaspoon cinnamon
¼ teaspoon nutmeg
1 egg

2 tablespoons soft shortening
½ cup currants
¼ cup cut-up citron

Quick White Icing:
1 cup confectioners sugar,
 sifted
1 tablespoon water or milk,
 or 1½ tablespoons cream
½ teaspoon vanilla

In a mixing bowl, dissolve the yeast in very warm water. Stir in the sugar, half of the flour, the salt, and spices. Beat with a spoon until smooth. Add the egg and shortening. Beat in the rest of the flour, the currants, and citron. Scrape down the sides; cover with a cloth. Let rise in a warm place (85°) until double, about 30 minutes. Stir down; spoon into greased muffin cups, filling ½ full. Let rise in a warm place until the dough reaches the tops of the cups, 20-30 minutes. Bake at 400° for 15-20 minutes. Make a cross on each with **Quick White Icing**.

Quick White Icing: Combine the sugar with water, milk, or cream and stir to spreadable consistency. Stir in the vanilla.

Makes 12 large or 18 medium-size buns.

Simplicity Carmel Rolls

2 loaves frozen bread dough
   (white, cinnamon, or raisin)
2 cups brown sugar, packed
½ cup whipping cream

1 cup pecans
Salad oil, melted butter,
  or margarine
½ cup granulated sugar
3 tablespoons cinnamon

Allow the frozen bread dough to thaw in the original wrapping. Let it rise until doubled in size. Grease the sides only of a 9x13-inch aluminum baking pan. Mix the brown sugar and whipping cream together until smooth. Spread the mixture into the bottom of the baking pan. Sprinkle with ½ cup pecans. Place the dough on a pastry sheet and roll or pat into a 12x14-inch rectangle about ½-inch thick. Brush slightly with the salad oil, melted butter, or margarine.Combine the granulated sugar and cinnamon until well blended; spread evenly over the dough to within 1 inch of the edges. Chop the remaining ½ cup pecans and sprinkle over the dough. Roll dough tightly into a roll and seal. Cut into 12 (1-inch) slices and place in the carmel-nut mixture in the baking pan. Let rise until double in size. Bake at 350° for 20-25 minutes. Do not overbake or the carmel will harden. To remove, invert onto waxed paper.

Makes 12 large rolls.

Blueberry Muffins

2 cups all-purpose flour
1 ½ teaspoons salt
4 teaspoons baking powder
⅔ cup sugar
1 ½ cups whole wheat flour

4 eggs
½ cup melted butter
1 ½ cups milk
2 cups blueberries

Sift together the flour, salt, baking powder, and sugar. Stir in the whole wheat flour. In another bowl, beat the eggs until light, then add the melted butter. Add the milk. Stir the egg mixture into the flour mixture quickly. Toss the blueberries in a little flour, then fold them into the batter. Bake in greased muffin tins at 450° for 15 minutes or until done.

This is the secret of good muffins: don't overdo the mixing—the minute the ingredients are combined, stop! Muffins freeze well. Reheat slowly until piping hot.

Makes 3 dozen large muffins.

Pancakes

Brussels Waffles á la Katherine

4 egg yolks
2 cups unsifted flour
1½ cups milk
6 tablespoons butter, melted
1 teaspoon salt

1 teaspoon vanilla
6 egg whites, stiffly beaten
Whipped cream
Strawberries

Beat the egg yolks until light and lemon colored. Add the flour alternately with the milk. This should make a soft, smooth batter. Add the butter, salt, and vanilla. Mix well. Fold in the egg whites. Bake in a hot waffle iron. Serve with whipped cream and strawberries. During fresh strawberry season, sprinkle with powdered sugar and add fresh sliced strawberries and whipped cream. During the rest of the year substitute frozen strawberries, partially thawed. Non-dairy whipped topping may be used instead of whipped cream, if desired.

Serves 6 to 8.

Feathery Buttermilk Pancakes

1 cup sifted flour
½ teaspoon salt
½ teaspoon baking soda
¾ teaspoon baking powder

1 egg
2 teaspoons sugar
3 tablespoons oil
1 cup buttermilk

Sift together the flour, salt, baking soda, and baking powder. Beat the egg with the sugar until thick; add the oil gradually, while beating. Combine with the buttermilk. Gradually stir the egg-milk mixture into the flour mixture, blending well. Pour the batter onto a greased hot griddle or an electric frying pan at 350°. Use about 2 tablespoons for each pancake. When bubbles appear on the cakes and they are browned on the bottom, turn and brown the other side. Do not turn a second time. Serve hot, with fresh fruit sauce, applesauce, maple syrup, or honey.

Makes 14 (5-inch) pancakes.

Popover Pancakes

½ cup flour
½ cup milk
2 eggs
¼ cup butter (½ stick)

2 tablespoons confectioners
   sugar
Juice of ½ lemon
Honey, jam, or marmalade

In a mixing bowl, combine the flour, milk, and eggs. Beat lightly, leaving the batter slightly lumpy. In a 12x8-inch oval top-of-the-stove au gratin dish or a 12-inch round skillet with heatproof handle, heat the butter until very hot. Pour in the batter. Bake at 425° for 20 minutes or until the pancake is puffed all around the sides of the dish or skillet and golden brown. Remove from the oven and sprinkle with confectioners sugar and lemon juice. Return to the oven for 2-3 minutes, or until the pancake is glazed. Serve immediately with honey, jam, or marmalade.

Try this with sugared strawberries during the fresh strawberry season. Yummy!

Serves 2 to 4.

Trey's Orange French Toast

2 eggs, lightly beaten
1 teaspoon fresh grated
   orange peel
Dash gound nutmeg

¼ cup fresh squeezed
   orange juice
4 slices bread
Butter or margarine

In a shallow dish, combine the eggs, orange peel, nutmeg, and juice. Dip the bread slices, one at a time, into the egg mixture. In a skillet, brown the bread on both sides in butter.

Serves 2.

Larry's Hamburger Pancakes

3 egg yolks
½ pound ground beef
   (Larry uses regular
   ground beef)
¼ teaspoon baking powder

½ teaspoon salt
¼ teaspoon pepper
1 tablespoon lemon juice
1 tablespoon minced parsley
1 tablespoon minced onion
3 egg whites, stiffly beaten

Blend together the egg yolks, ground beef, baking power, salt, pepper, lemon juice, minced parsley, and minced onion. Fold in the egg whites. Drop by spoonfuls onto a greased, hot griddle or skillet. When puffed and brown, turn and brown the other side. Serve at once.

Serves 2 to 4.

Condiments

Port Wine Jelly

2 cups red port wine
1-inch piece of stick cinnamon
1 small piece of dried or
  fresh ginger root

3 whole cloves
3 cups sugar
½ bottle liquid pectin

Combine in a saucepan the wine, cinnamon, ginger, and cloves. Simmer 5 minutes. Strain. Combine the spiced wine and sugar in the top of a double boiler. Place over boiling water and stir until the sugar is dissolved. Cover and let heat for 5 minutes. Add the pectin; stir well. Remove from boiling water and skim if necessary. Pour into sterilized glasses or jars. Cover with paraffin.

This jelly is excellent with meat. Try a spoonful as a topping for fruit salad and cottage cheese, or make a sophisticated peanut butter and jelly sandwich.

*To use as a **Ham Sauce:** Mix ¼ cup spiced jelly with ⅛ teaspoon dry mustard and 1½ teaspoons vinegar in a small saucepan. Heat, stirring constantly, until jelly is melted and blended. Serve warm with ham.*

Makes 5 (6 ounce) glasses.

Honeydew Melon and Peach Conserve

4 cups peeled & diced
  honeydew melon
4 cups diced peaches
4 cups sugar
2 cups light corn syrup
4 tablespoons lemon juice

2 tablespoons butter
1 cup broken walnut meats
1 teaspoon grated orange rind
½ teaspoon nutmeg
¼ teaspoon salt

Cook the honeydew melon and peaches together 20 minutes over low heat. Stir to prevent sticking. Add the sugar, syrup, and lemon juice. Add the butter to eliminate foam. Boil rapidly for 40 minutes. Add the walnuts, orange rind, nutmeg, and salt. Boil 3 minutes. Pour into hot, sterilized jars. Seal or paraffin at once.

Cantaloupe may be substituted for honeydew melon.

233

Oregon Grape Jelly

Wash 2 quarts of grape berries; place in a preserving kettle and barely cover with water. Cook about 10 minutes; mash well to release juice, and cook a few minutes longer. Put through a colander to remove the seeds and skins; then let the juice drip through a jelly bag. Measure the juice and heat to boiling. Add ¾ cup sugar to each cup juice. Stir until sugar is dissolved; boil rapidly until jelly stage is reached. Pour into hot sterilized glasses and seal with paraffin.

Those little clusters of blue berries growing on a low shrub with holly-like leaves are Oregon Grapes, particularly prized for flavor in jelly.

Frozen Strawberry and Fresh Peach Jam

*1 (10 ounce) package frozen
  sliced strawberries
6-8 peaches, peeled, sliced
  & chopped*

*¼ cup lemon juice
1 (1¾ ounce) box dry
  fruit pectin
6 cups sugar*

Thaw the frozen sliced strawberries, and place in a 4 cup container. Peel, slice and chop enough peaches to fill the container. Place the fruit into a 6 or 8 quart saucepan. Add the lemon juice and dry fruit pectin, and mix with the fruit in the saucepan. Place over high heat, and stir until the mixture comes to a hard boil. Boil for 1 minute. At once add sugar. Bring to a full rolling boil (a boil that can not be stirred down.). Boil hard 1 minute, stirring constantly. Remove from the heat. Skim off the foam with a metal spoon. Stir and skim 5 minutes to cool slightly and to prevent floating fruit. Ladle into sterilized jars or glasses. Seal.

Makes approximately 6 cups.

Spicy Plum Jam

4 cups washed, halved, &
   pitted plums
2 cups sugar
¼ teaspoon ground cinnamon
⅛ teaspoon ground cloves

⅛ teaspoon ground allspice
⅛ teaspoon ground ginger
⅛ teaspoon dry mustard
¼ cup vinegar

Combine the prepared plums with the sugar, cinnamon, cloves, allspice, ginger, dry mustard, and vinegar. Cook over medium heat, stirring frequently to prevent sticking. When desired thickness has been reached, seal at once in hot, sterilized standard jars.

Makes 2 pints.

Old-Fashioned Apple Butter

1 gallon apple cider
4 quarts peeled, cored, &
   sliced apples (about 7
   pounds; Jonathan or Winesap
   have best flavor)

1 pound granulated sugar
1 cup dark brown sugar
1 teaspoon ground cinnamon
1 teaspoon ground cloves
1 teaspoon ground allspice

Pour the apple cider into a large (about 4 gallon) heavy enamel kettle, set on to boil; then boil, uncovered, until the volume is reduced by half. Add the apples, a few at a time, stirring all the while. Boil, uncovered, until all the pieces of apple disappear and the mixture is thick and glossy. (*You'll have to stir constantly to prevent sticking.*) Stir in the granulated sugar, brown sugar, cinnamon, cloves, and allspice; then remove the apple butter from the heat. Continue to stir until sugars are completely dissolved. Ladle into hot, sterilized pint-size preserving jars, filling to within ⅛-inch of the top. Seal; process for 10 minutes in a simmering water bath. Cool; then store on a cool, dry shelf.

Apricot Orange Jam

7 pounds apricots, seeds
    removed (about 14 cups)
5 pounds sugar (10 cups)

Grated rind of 1 orange
Juice of 3 oranges
2½ cups crushed pineapple

Mix all ingredients thoroughly. Cook, stirring carefully, as jam thickens. Test by sampling. Place a spoonful of jam on a cool plate. Cook until desired thickness is reached. It will require about 1 hour of cooking. Pour into sterilized jars, and seal while hot.

Makes 8 to 8½ pints.

Frozen Fresh Red Raspberry Jam

3 cups finely mashed or
    sieved red raspberries
6 cups sugar

1 box powdered pectin
1 cup water

Combine the fruit and sugar. Let stand about 20 minutes, stirring occasionally. Boil the powdered pectin and water rapidly for 1 minute, stirring constantly. Remove from the heat. Add the fruit and stir about 2 minutes. Pour into jars and tighten the lids. Let stand at room temperature from 24 to 48 hours or until jelled. Store in the freezer or refrigerator.

Liquid pectin can be used in this jam. Omit the powdered pectin and water and use ½ cup liquid pectin. No heating is necessary.

Christmas Jam

1 (11 ounce) package
    dried apricots
1 (30 ounce) can
    pineapple chunks

3½ cups water
1 (8 ounce) jar maraschino
    cherries
6 cups sugar

In a large saucepan, combine the apricots, pineapple and syrup, water and cherry syrup. Let stand 1 hour. Cook slowly until the apricots are tender. Add the sugar and cook slowly, stirring often, until thick and clear (216° on a candy-jelly thermometer). Add the cherries, cut into quarters, and cook a few minutes longer (220°). Pour into hot, sterilized jars and cover with melted paraffin.

Makes 6 cups.

Tomato Preserves

6 cups ripe tomatoes
6¾ cups sugar

1 lemon, thinly sliced
½ teaspoon ground ginger

Skin and remove all core portions of the tomatoes. Cut them up, and measure 6 cups. Cook, simmering, 10 minutes to evaporate some moisture. Add the sugar; stir until dissolved. Remove any seeds from the lemon and add the slices to the tomato and sugar. Add the ginger. Stir frequently. Simmer and stir about 45 minutes or until the desired thickness is reached. Pour into hot, sterilized jars. Fill to ¼-inch of the top. Seal at once.

Makes about 6 cups.

Zucchini Relish

10 cups grated zucchini
4 cups grated onion
2 large green peppers,
   chopped
1 large red pepper, chopped
1 carrot, grated

¼ cup salt
2 cups vinegar
4 cups sugar
1½ teaspoons black pepper
1 teaspoon ground nutmeg
1 teaspoon turmeric

Place the zucchini, onion, peppers, carrot, and salt in a glass bowl, and let stand overnight. Drain, rinse with cold water, and drain well again. Add the remaining ingredients, and bring to a boil. Boil 5 minutes. Place in clean, hot jars, leaving ¼-inch head space. Wipe the lip of the jar clean, attach the lid and ring, and tighten. Place in a boiling water bath for 10 minutes. Remove the jars, and allow to cool away from drafts. Check the seal.

This is made quick and easy when you use the food processor to prepare the vegetables.

Makes about 5 pints.

Green Tomato Mincemeat

3 pounds green tomatoes
3½ pounds apples
2 pounds brown sugar
1 pound seeded raisins
1 tablespoon salt
1 cup ground suet (optional)

1¼ cups vinegar
2½ tablespoons cinnamon
2 teaspoons cloves
1 tablespoon nutmeg
1 tablespoon lemon rind
3 tablespoons lemon juice

Wash, stem, and quarter the green tomatoes. Put the tomatoes through a food chopper or finely chop by hand. Drain and discard the liquid. Put in a large kettle, cover with cold water, place over heat, bring to a boil, and simmer for 5 minutes. Drain well. Peel, core, and grind the apples. Combine with the tomatoes and add the remaining ingredients. Place over heat and simmer, stirring frequently, about 35 minutes. Place in sterilized jars and seal.

Note: Fresh apples may be added to mincemeat when pies are made.

Makes 8 pints.

Iced Green Tomato Pickles

3 cups lime (air slacked or
   agriculture lime)
2 gallons water
7 pounds green tomatoes,
   cored & sliced
Fresh water
5 pounds sugar
3 pints vinegar

1 teaspoon cloves
1 teaspoon ginger
1 teaspoon allspice
1 teaspoon celery seed
1 teaspoon mace
1 teaspoon cinnamon
1 cup raisins (optional)

Dissolve the lime in the water. Soak the tomatoes in the lime-water mixture for 24 hours. Drain and soak in fresh water for 4 hours, changing the water, rinsing thoroughly every hour. Drain thoroughly. Place the sugar, vinegar, and spices in a kettle. Bring this syrup to boiling, pour over the tomatoes, and let stand overnight. In the morning, boil for an hour, then seal in sterilized jars. Raisins may be added about 10 minutes before canning if desired.

The lime makes the tomatoes very crisp, hence the name "Iced." The pickles are wonderful and very unusual.

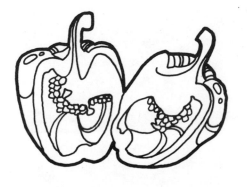

Desserts

Cakes & Frostings

Wenatchee Apple Cake

4 cups finely diced apples
2 cups granulated sugar
½ cup oil
2 eggs, beaten
2 cups flour, unsifted

2 teaspoons cinnamon
2 teaspoons soda
½ teaspoon salt
2 teaspoons vanilla
1 cup chopped nuts

Place the apples in a large bowl. Add the sugar, and let stand ½ hour. Add the oil and beaten eggs. Sift in the flour, cinnamon, soda, and salt. Blend in the vanilla and chopped nuts. Place in a greased and floured 9x13x2-inch pan and bake at 350° for 40 minutes. Serve with whipped cream, ice cream, or plain.

Serves 6 to 8.

Pumpkin Spice Cake

½ cup shortening
1 cup brown sugar
2 eggs
¾ cup sieved pumpkin
2 cups sifted flour
2 teaspoons baking powder
½ teaspoon salt

½ teaspoon baking soda
½ teaspoon cinnamon
½ teaspoon nutmeg
½ teaspoon allspice
½ cup sour milk
½ cup chopped nuts

Cream the shortening with the brown sugar. Add the eggs, one at a time, and beat until fluffy. Add the pumpkin. Sift the flour with the baking powder, salt, soda, and seasonings. Add the dry ingredients alternately with the sour milk. Add the nuts. Pour into two 9-inch pans or one 13x9½x2-inch pan, greased and floured. Bake at 350° for 25-30 minutes for the 2 layers, or 40-45 minutes for the loaf pan.

Serves 8 to 10.

Cocoa Apple Cake

3 eggs
2 cups sugar
1 cup butter or margarine
½ cup water
2½ cups flour
2 tablespoons cocoa
1 teaspoon baking soda

1 teaspoon cinnamon
1 teaspoon allspice
1 cup chopped nuts
½ cup chocolate chips
2 cups apples, cored &
  finely chopped
1 tablespoon vanilla

Beat together the eggs, sugar, butter or margarine, and water until fluffy. Sift together the flour, cocoa, soda, cinnamon, and allspice. Add to the creamed mixture, mixing well. Fold in the finely chopped nuts, chocolate chips, apples, and vanilla until evenly distributed. Spoon into a greased and floured 10-inch loose bottom tube pan. Bake at 325° for 60-70 minutes or until the cake tests done.

Serves 10.

Crème De Menthe Cake

1 (18½ ounce) deluxe white
  cake mix
4 large eggs
1 (3¾ ounce) package instant
  vanilla pudding and pie mix
½ cup orange juice

½ cup vegetable oil
¼ cup green crème de menthe
¼ cup water
¼ teaspoon vanilla
1 (5½ ounce) can chocolate
  syrup

Grease and flour a large bundt* pan. Combine the cake mix, eggs, pudding mix, orange juice, vegetable oil, green crème de menthe, water, and vanilla. Beat 4 minutes. Divide the mixture into ⅔ and ⅓. Pour the ⅔ into the prepared pan. Mix the chocolate syrup into the remaining ⅓ batter and pour over the batter in the pan. Bake at 350° for 35-45 minutes. Set on a wire rack and cool in the pan.

*A 10-inch tube cake pan, greased and floured, can be substituted for a bundt pan.

Serves 10 to 12.

Carrot Cake

2 cups granulated sugar
1½ cups vegetable oil
2 teaspoons vanilla
4 eggs
2½ cups flour
2 teaspoons baking soda
1 teaspoon salt
2 teaspoons cinnamon
1 (15¼ ounce) can crushed
  pineapple

3 cups peeled &
  grated carrots
1 cut chopped walnuts

Cream Cheese Frosting:
1 (8 ounce) package
  cream cheese
½ cup butter
1 pound box powdered sugar
1 tablespoon vanilla extract

Combine the sugar with the vegetable oil and vanilla. Beat until light and fluffy. Add the eggs, one at a time; continue beating until light and well mixed. Combine the flour (unsifted), with the soda, salt, and cinnamon; sift and set aside. Drain the pineapple in a fine sieve, stirring to completely drain. This will measure ¾ cup crushed pineapple. Add the flour, carrots, and pineapple alternately to the creamed mixture. Mix in the chopped walnuts. Place in a greased and floured 13x9x2-inch cake pan. Bake at 350° for 45-50 minutes or until it tests done. Cool 10 minutes in the pan on a rack. Remove from the pan and complete the cooling on the rack. Frost with **Cream Cheese Frosting.**

Cream Cheese Frosting: Allow the cream cheese and butter to soften. Cream together with the powdered sugar and vanilla.

Serves 12 to 15.

Chocolate Zucchini Cake

2½ cups unsifted all-purpose
    flour
½ cup unsweetened cocoa
2½ teaspoons baking powder
1½ teaspoons baking soda
1 teaspoon salt
1 teaspoon cinnamon
¾ cup butter
2 cups sugar
3 eggs
2 cups grated, unpeeled
    zucchini (about ½ pound)

2 teaspoons grated
    orange peel
2 teaspoons vanilla
½ cup milk
1 cup finely chopped walnuts

Orange Glaze:
¾ cup confectioners sugar
1 tablespoon orange juice
½ teaspoon grated orange
    peel

Combine the flour (measured by spooning into a cup) in a bowl with the cocoa, baking powder, baking soda, salt, and cinnamon. Sift and set aside. In a large mixer bowl, cream the butter with the mixer at medium speed. Beat until light. Add the eggs, one at a time, and continue beating until well mixed. Stir in the grated zucchini, orange peel, and vanilla. Alternately stir in the dry ingredients, milk, and walnuts. Pour into a greased and floured pan. If using a 12- cup bundt pan, bake at 350° for 1 hour or until a toothpick inserted in the center comes out clean, or bake in a 13x9x2-inch cake pan at 350° for 45 minutes or until done. Let cool in the pan on a wire rack for 15 minutes. Invert to remove. Spread with **Orange Glaze** while the cake is still warm.

Orange Glaze: Combine the confectioners sugar, orange juice, and orange peel, stirring until smooth. Add a little more orange juice if necessary. Spread on the cake.

Serves 16.

Peanut Butter Cake with Crunch Topping

¾ cup peanut butter
½ cup vegetable shortening
1 ½ teaspoons vanilla extract
2 ¼ cups light brown sugar,
   firmly packed
3 eggs
3 cups all-purpose flour
3 teaspoons baking powder
½ teaspoon salt
1 ¼ cups milk

Crunch Topping:
½ cup flaked coconut
6 tablespoons butter
2 egg yolks
⅓ cup light cream
2 teaspoons vanilla extract
1 pound sifted confectioners
   sugar
½ cup finely chopped peanuts

Cream the peanut butter, vegetable shortening, and vanilla. Beat in the brown sugar. Add the eggs, one at a time, beating after each addition. Mix the flour, baking powder, and salt. Alternately add the dry ingredients to the creamed mixture with the milk, beginning and ending with the dry ingredients. Bake in 3 greased and floured 9-inch layer cake pans at 350° for 30-35 minutes or until the cake shrinks from the sides of the pan. Cool the layers on a rack, and then frost with the **Crunch Topping.**

Crunch Topping: Stir the coconut in a skillet over low heat until golden brown. Cool. Mash the butter until soft and fluffy. Beat in the egg yolks, cream, and vanilla. Gradually beat in enough confectioners sugar to make the frosting the right spreading consistency. In a small bowl, mix together the coconut and peanuts. Spread some of the frosting between the cake layers, sprinkling some of the peanut-coconut mixture over the frosting. Frost the sides and top of the cake, and sprinkle with the remaining peanut-coconut mixture.

Peanut Butter Cake

¾ cup softened butter
¾ cup peanut butter
2 cups brown sugar,
   firmly packed
1 teaspoon vanilla
3 eggs
2 cups all-purpose flour
1 tablespoon baking powder
½ teaspoon salt
1 cup milk

½ cup chopped nuts

Fudgy Frosting:
1 (6 ounce) package semi-
   sweet chocolate chips
⅓ cup milk
1½ cups confectioners sugar

Cream the softened butter with the peanut butter and brown sugar until light and fluffy. Stir in the vanilla. Add the eggs, one at a time, mixing well after each addition. Sift together the flour, baking powder, and salt; add to the creamed mixture alternately with the milk. Mix well. Pour into a buttered 13x9-inch baking pan. Bake at 350° for 45-50 minutes or until a wooden pick inserted in the center comes out clean. Cool. Spread with **Fudgy Frosting.** Sprinkle with the chopped nuts.

Fudgy Frosting: Combine the chocolate chips and milk; melt over low heat, stirring to blend. Add the sugar; beat until smooth.

Serves 10 to 12.

14 Minute Fruit Cake

½ cup shortening
1⅓ cups sugar
2 eggs
1 cup mincemeat
2 cups all-purpose flour
1½ tablespoons cocoa
2 teaspoons baking powder
½ teaspoon salt
½ cup milk
⅓ cup chopped nuts

2 cups diced candied fruit mix
   or 1 (1 pound) package
   diced fruit mix

Cream Cheese Frosting:
3 ounces cream cheese
3 cups powdered sugar
2 tablespoons orange
  marmalade
1-2 tablespoons lemon juice
Orange juice

Cream the shortening and sugar, adding the eggs, one at a time, and beating thoroughly. Heat the mincemeat until the suet is melted. Add to the creamed mixture while warm. Sift the flour, cocoa, baking powder, and salt. Add alternately to the creamed mixture with the milk. Add the chopped nuts and candied fruit mix. Pour into two greased 8-inch layer pans and bake at 350° for 35-40 minutes or until done. Frost with **Cream Cheese Frosting.**

Cream Cheese Frosting: Combine all ingredients, adding just enough orange juice to moisten.

Serves 10 to 15.

249

Banana Cheese Cake

¾ cup graham cracker
   crumbs
2 tablespoons brown sugar
3 tablespoons butter
   or margarine
¼ teaspoon nutmeg or
   cinnamon

Filling:
1 tablespoon gelatin

½ cup water
2 eggs, separated
¼ cup sugar
8 ounces cream cheese or
   cottage cheese
1 tablespoon lemon juice
¼ teaspoon salt
¼ cup heavy cream, whipped
2 ripe bananas

Combine the graham cracker crumbs, brown sugar, butter or margarine, and nutmeg or cinnamon. Mix well until blended. Measure off and reserve ¼ cup of this mixture for the topping. Place the remaining crumbs in a pan (8-inch or 9-inch spring-form cake pan). Cover with waxed paper, and press firmly and evenly against the bottom and sides to form a crust.

Filling: Soften the gelatin in half the water (¼ cup). Combine the egg yolks, which have been slightly beaten, with the sugar and the remaining portion of water (¼ cup). Place in the top of a double boiler over hot water, not boiling water, or use low temperature cooking. Heat and stir until thickened. Stir in the softened gelatin until dissolved. Beat the egg whites until stiff. Remove the thickened egg mixture from heat. Beat the cream cheese or cottage cheese until soft and creamy. Add the gelatin mixture, lemon juice, and salt, beating constantly. Fold in the beaten egg whites and whipped cream. Allow to stand until partially set. Slice the bananas. Place a thin layer of filling on the crumb crust. Arrange a layer of bananas on top of the filling. Repeat layers, ending with filling. Top with the reserved crumbs. Refrigerate until completely set—about 2 hours.

Serves 6 to 8.

Four Sons Devil's Food Cake

½ cup butter
1 pound brown sugar
2 eggs, beaten
2 squares unsweetened
    chocolate, melted

½ cup buttermilk
2 teaspoons vanilla
2¼ cups sifted cake flour
½ teaspoon salt
2 teaspoons baking soda
1 cup boiling water

Cream the butter and brown sugar. Add the eggs, beating hard. Stir in the melted chocolate, buttermilk, and vanilla. Gradually add the cake flour, sifted with salt, beating well after each addition. Last, stir the soda into the boiling water, then into the batter. This batter is very thin. Pour into a greased and floured 9x13x2-inch pan or 2 layer pans. Bake at 375° for 15 minutes, then reduce heat and continue baking at 350° for 20-30 minutes more.

Serves 4 boys.

Chocolate Chip Cake

1 cup uncooked oatmeal
1¾ cups boiling water
½ cup soft margarine
1 cup brown sugar, packed
1 cup granulated sugar
2 eggs
1¾ cups unsifted flour

1 teaspoon baking soda
½ teaspoon salt
1 tablespoon cocoa
1 (6 ounce) package semi-
    sweet chocolate chips
¾ cup chopped nuts

Cover the uncooked oatmeal with the boiling water in a large bowl. Let it set for 10 minutes. Add the margarine and mix until melted. Add the brown sugar and the granulated sugar. Mix well. Add the eggs, one at a time, and beat well. Sift together the flour, soda, salt, and cocoa. Stir until well blended. Add ½ package or ½ cup semi-sweet chocate chips. Spread the mixture evenly in a greased and floured 9x13x2-inch pan. Sprinkle ½ cup chocolate chips and the chopped nuts over the top. Bake at 350° for 40-45 minutes.

Variation: Coconut may be substituted for nuts.

Serves 8 to 10.

251

Oatmeal Cake with Broiled Topping

1 cup oatmeal
1⅓ cups hot water
1 cup brown sugar
1 cup granulated sugar
½ cup cooking oil
1⅓ cups all purpose flour,
  unsifted
2 tablespoons wheat germ
1 teaspoon nutmeg

1 teaspoon cinnamon
1 teaspoon soda
½ teaspoon salt

Broiled Topping:
1 cup brown sugar
⅔ cup coconut
⅔ cup nutmeats
½ cup butter
3 tablespoons cream

Place the oatmeal in a bowl, add the hot water, and set aside. Combine the brown sugar, granulated sugar, and cooking oil. Blend in the flour, wheat germ, nutmeg, cinnamon, soda, and salt. Mix thoroughly, then add the oatmeal. Pour into a greased and floured 9x13x2-inch pan. Bake at 350° for 35-40 minutes or until done. Remove from the oven and spread with **Broiled Topping.**

Broiled Topping: Combine all ingredients. Spread the topping on the cake and toast under the broiler. Watch carefully!!

Serves 10 to 12.

Pineapple Skillet Cake

½ cup butter
½ cup brown sugar
5 slices canned pineapple,
   drained
5 maraschino cherries
A few whole pecans,
   if desired
1 (18½ ounce) package
   yellow cake mix

1 (3¾ ounce) package
   vanilla pudding mix
½ cup apple juice
1 teaspoon rum extract
½ cup vegetable oil
4 eggs, lightly beaten
Whipped cream

Melt the butter in a heavy 10-inch skillet. Add the brown sugar and blend well. Spread evenly over the skillet. Arrange the slices of canned pineapple, drained, over the sugar. Place a cherry in the center of each slice. Scatter a few whole pecans over the sugar, if desired. Combine the package of yellow cake mix with the package of vanilla pudding mix, apple juice, rum extract, vegetable oil, and eggs. Beat well with an electric mixer for 2 minutes (or for 6 minutes by hand). Pour the batter over the pineapple/sugar combination and bake at 350° for 50-60 minutes or until the cake tests done. Allow to cool 5 minutes before inverting onto a serving plate. Serve with whipped cream, if desired.

Serves 6 to 8.

Cookies

Apple Spice Bars

½ cup shortening
1 cup sugar
1 egg
1 teaspoon vanilla
2 cups flour
2 teaspoons baking powder
1 teaspoon salt

1 teaspoon cinnamon
1 teaspoon nutmeg
2 tablespoons cocoa
⅔ cup milk
½ teaspoon baking soda
1 ½ cups diced raw apple
Powdered sugar

Cream the shortening and the sugar until fluffy. Add the egg and the vanilla. Beat well. Sift the flour and measure 2 cups, and then sift again three times with the baking powder, salt, cinnamon, nutmeg, and cocoa. Add to the creamed mixture with the milk in which you dissolve the soda. Add the diced raw apple. Pour into a greased and floured 13x9x2-inch pan or 3 (8-inch) cake pans. Bake at 350° for 25 minutes or until the cookies test done. When cool, cut into 1x3-inch bars and roll in powdered sugar.

Makes 2½ dozen bars.

Peanut Butter—Chocolate Chip Bars

2 eggs
⅓ cup water
¼ cup butter or margarine,
   softened

1 cup crunchy peanut butter
1 package yellow cake mix
1 (12 ounce) package semi-
   sweet chocolate chips

Beat the eggs, water, butter or margarine, peanut butter, and half a package yellow cake mix (dry) until light and fluffy. Stir in the remaining cake mix and the chocolate chips. The dough will be stiff. Spread in a greased and floured 15½x10½x1-inch jelly roll pan. Bake at 375° for about 20 minutes. Cool; cut into bars.

Makes about 30 (3x1½-inch) bars.

255

Cream Cheese Cookies

⅓ cup butter
⅓ cup firmly packed
   brown sugar
1 cup flour
½ cup chopped walnuts
   or pecans

Filling:
¼ cup granulated sugar
1 (8 ounce) package cream
   cheese, softened
1 egg
2 tablespoons milk
1 tablespoon lemon juice
½ teaspoon vanilla

Cream the butter and brown sugar, then add the flour and chopped walnuts or pecans. Combine to make a crumb mixture. Reserve 1 cup crumb mixture for a topping. Press the remaining crumb mixture into a buttered 8-inch square pan. Bake at 350° for 12 to 15 minutes.

Filling: Blend the granulated sugar with the cream cheese. Mix well, then add the egg. Continue beating and add the milk, lemon juice, and vanilla. Combine all ingredients well. Spread this mixture over the top of the crust when it comes from the oven. Sprinkle on the remaining crumbs. Bake at 350° for 25 minutes more. Cool. Cut into squares. Refrigerate.

Makes 24 cookies.

Pecan Bars

½ cup butter or margarine
1½ cup dark brown sugar
½ teaspoon salt
1 cup plus 2 tablespoons
   sifted flour
2 tablespoons milk

2 eggs
1 teaspoon vanilla extract
½ teaspoon baking powder
1 (4 ounce) can shredded
   coconut
1 cup chopped pecans

Work the butter in a bowl until creamy; add ½ cup brown sugar and salt; beat until fluffy. Blend in 1 cup flour and milk. Pat into the bottom of a greased 9x9x2-inch pan. Bake at 325° for 20 minutes. Cool slightly. Beat the eggs well; add the 1 cup brown sugar and vanilla. Blend in the 2 tablespoons flour and baking powder. Fold in the coconut and pecans. Pour over the baked layer in the pan. Bake for 35 minutes more.   Cool slightly, and cut into 1½ -inch squares.

Makes 3 dozen.

Cheesecake Cookies

¾ cup butter
1 cup brown sugar
1 teaspoon vanilla
1½ cups sifted flour
1 teaspoon salt
½ teaspoon baking soda
1 teaspoon cinnamon
¾ cup quick-cooking
    oatmeal, uncooked
¾ cup chopped pecans
1 cup flaked coconut

Filling:
1 can sweetened
    condensed milk
¼ teaspoon salt
½ cup lemon juice
1 tablespoon grated
    lemon peel
2 eggs, slightly beaten

Beat the butter until fluffy, then gradually blend in the brown sugar, then the vanilla. Sift together the flour, salt, baking soda, and cinnamon. Stir into the butter mixture, then add the oatmeal, and blend to make a crumb mixture. Fold in the chopped pecans and coconut. Press ½ of the crumb mixture into a 13x9x2-inch pan. Set aside while preparing the **Filling**. Pour the **Filling** over the crumb mixture. Top with the remaining crumbs. Bake at 350° for 25-30 minutes. Cool thoroughly in the baking pan.

Filling: Mix the sweetened condensed milk, salt, lemon juice, and lemon peel, and stir until thickened. Blend in the eggs.

Makes 4 dozen squares.

257

Butterscotch-Coconut Bars

¾ cup butter or margarine
1 cup dark brown sugar,
   firmly packed
1 egg
1 tablespoon grated
   orange peel
2 cups sifted flour

¾ teaspoon salt
½ teaspoon baking powder
½ teaspoon baking soda
¼ cup orange juice
1 (6 ounce) package
   butterscotch chips
1 cup flaked coconut

Cream together the butter and brown sugar. Beat in the egg and orange peel. Sift together the flour, salt, baking powder, and baking soda. Add alternately to the creamed mixture with the orange juice. Stir in the butterscotch chips and coconut. Spread evenly in a greased 9x13x2-inch baking pan. Bake at 350° for 30 minutes. Cool, then cut into 1½-inch squares.

Makes about 4 dozen bars.

Pecan Squares

½ cup softened butter
1½ cups dark brown sugar
½ teaspoon salt
1 cup flour
2 tablespoons sherry
2 eggs

1 teaspoon vanilla
2 tablespoons flour
½ teaspoon baking powder
1 cup chopped pecans
1 cup flaked coconut

Combine the softened butter, ½ cup brown sugar, and salt. Beat until fluffy. Blend in the flour and sherry. Pat into a greased 9x9x2-inch pan. Bake 20 minutes at 350°. Cool slightly. Beat the eggs well and add 1 cup brown sugar and vanilla. Blend in the flour and baking powder. Fold in the pecans and coconut. Pour over the baked layer in the pan and bake 35 minutes. Cool slightly and cut into 1½-inch squares.

Makes 36 squares.

Mystery Chocolate Balls

1 (6 ounce) package semi-
   sweet chocolate chips
2 sticks (9¼ or 11 ounce)
   pie crust mix

2 teaspoons vanilla
½ cup finely chopped walnuts
   or pecans
¾ cup cocoa
¾ cup confectioners sugar

Melt the chocolate chips in the top of a double boiler over hot (not boiling) water. Remove the pan from the water. Gradually blend in the pie crust mix, stirring until smooth after each addition. Add the vanilla and nuts, mixing until well blended. (If the dough is soft and sticking to your hands, chill it briefly in the refrigerator, but don't let it get too hard!) Shape the dough into marble-sized balls (a scant 1-inch and no bigger). Place on ungreased baking sheets. Bake at 400° for 10 minutes. Meantime, mix the cocoa and confectioners sugar. Sift into a large mixing bowl. Remove the baked cookies from the oven and let stand for 5 minutes, then roll carefully in the cocoa-sugar mixture. When thoroughly cold, roll again. Store any unused cocoa-sugar mixture in a covered jar for your next batch of cookies.

Makes 6 dozen cookies.

Fresh Apple Peanut Butter Cookies

½ cup shortening
½ cup peanut butter
½ cup granulated sugar
½ cup brown sugar, packed

1 egg
1½ cups all-purpose flour
¼ teaspoon baking soda
½ teaspoon baking powder
½ cup grated fresh apple

Cream together the shortening, peanut butter, granulated sugar, and brown sugar. Add the egg and beat well. Sift together the flour, soda, and baking powder. Blend with creamed mixture. Add the grated apple, stirring in well. Drop from a teaspoon onto an oiled cookie sheet. Place cookies 2 inches apart. Bake at 350° for 15 minutes or until done.

Makes 2½-3 dozen cookies.

Christy's Chewy Peanut Butter Bars

1 cup unsifted all-purpose
   flour
1 teaspoon baking powder
¼ teaspoon salt
⅔ cup old-fashioned
   peanut butter
¼ cup softened butter
   or margarine

¾ cup granulated sugar
¼ cup brown sugar,
   firmly packed
2 eggs
½ teaspoon vanilla
1 (6 ounce) package semi-
   sweet chocolate chips

Combine the flour, baking powder, and salt on wax paper. Stir to blend. Cream the peanut butter and butter thoroughly. Add the sugars gradually, beating until fluffy. Beat in the eggs, one at a time. Add the vanilla and blended dry ingredients to the creamed mixture. Stir in the chocolate chips. Spread the batter evenly in a greased 9-inch square pan. Bake at 350° for 30 minutes or until a wooden pick inserted in the center comes out almost clean. Cool in the pan on a rack. Cut into bars.

Makes 3 dozen bars.

Spiced Banana or Applesauce Bars

2 cups sifted all-purpose
   flour
2 teaspoons baking soda
1 teaspoon cinnamon
½ teaspoon nutmeg
¼ teaspoon cloves
½ cup soft butter or
   margarine

½ cup granulated sugar
½ cup brown sugar,
   firmly packed
1 egg
1 teaspoon vanilla
1½ cups mashed bananas
   or 1½ cups applesauce
1½ cups seedless raisins

Sift together the flour, soda, cinnamon, nutmeg, and cloves. Cream together the butter and sugars. Add the egg and vanilla, and beat until light. Gradually add the flour and mashed bananas or applesauce, or a combination of the two, and beat until combined. Blend in the raisins. Turn the mixture into a buttered and floured 15½x10½x1-inch pan. Bake at 350° for 25 minutes or just until the surface springs back when

260

gently pressed with fingertips. Cool the cake in the pan on a wire rack. Frost, if desired, with a butter/confectioners sugar frosting.

Makes about 4 dozen bars.

Seahawks Cookies

½ cup shortening
¾ cup granulated sugar
¼ cup brown sugar,
   firmly packed
2 eggs
1½ cups rolled oats
1½ cups unsifted all-
   purpose flour

¾ teaspoons baking powder
¼ teaspoon baking soda
1 teaspoon cinnamon
½ teaspoon ginger
½ teaspoon salt
½ cup milk
½ cup chopped walnuts
½ cup seedless raisins

Cream the shortening with the sugars until fluffy. Add the eggs, one at a time, and beat well after each addition. Stir in the rolled oats. Measure the unsifted flour and sift with the baking powder, baking soda, cinnamon, ginger, and salt. Stir into the first mixture alternately with the milk. Add the chopped walnuts and seedless raisins. Drop by rounded teaspoonfuls onto a greased baking sheet. Place the cookies 2 inches apart. Bake at 375° for 12-15 minutes or until golden brown. Remove the cookies to a cooling rack.

Makes 4½-5 dozen cookies.

Cream Cheese Date Bars

1 cup chopped dates
½ cup sugar
½ cup hot water
2 tablespoons lemon juice
2 tablespoons chopped
    walnuts

½ cup butter
1 (3 ounce) package
    cream cheese
2 cups flour
Salt

Soak the dates and sugar in the hot water for 8 minutes. Add the lemon juice and walnuts and set aside. Cream the butter and cream cheese. Gradually add the flour and a pinch of salt, mixing until crumbly. Press half the dough in a 7x11-inch pan, and spread on the date filling. Press the remaining dough on top. Bake at 400° for about 15 minutes.

Makes 2 dozen bars.

Honeymoon Bars

1 cup flour
½ cup brown sugar
½ cup butter
2 eggs, lightly beaten
1½ cups brown sugar
1 teaspoon vanilla
2 tablespoons flour
4 teaspoons baking powder

1 cup chopped walnuts
½ cup coconut

Frosting:
½ cup soft butter
1½ tablespoons lemon juice
1 teaspoon lemon rind
2 cups powdered sugar

Mix together the flour and brown sugar. Cut in the butter. Mix thoroughly and pat into a 9x12-inch pan. Bake at 325° for 15 minutes. Mix and spread over the first layer the eggs, brown sugar, vanilla, flour, baking powder, walnuts, and coconut. Bake at 325° for 25 minutes more or until the filling is set. Cool, frost, and cut into bars.

Frosting: Combine all ingredients. Spread evenly over the cooled cake.

Makes 30 bars.

Bourbon Balls

2½ cups finely crushed
    vanilla wafers
1 cup confectioners sugar
1 cup finely chopped nuts

2 tablespoons cocoa
3 tablespoons corn syrup
¼ cup bourbon

Mix the crushed vanilla wafers, confectioners sugar, nuts, and cocoa.
Add the corn syrup and bourbon. Mix with hands. Roll into 1-inch balls.
Roll in confectioners sugar to coat thoroughly.

Store in container with tight-fitting lid.

Makes 3 dozen.

Fruit & Puddings

Wenatchee Apple Crisp

2 pounds tart apples,
  peeled, cored &
  thickly sliced
⅓ cup apple brandy
Juice of ½ lemon
¾ cup flour

½ cup sugar
½ cup brown sugar
½ teaspoon nutmeg
½ teaspoon cinnamon
¼ teaspoon salt
½ cup sweet butter

Marinate the sliced apples in brandy and lemon juice for 30 minutes. In a large bowl, blend the remaining ingredients with fingertips until the mixture is in large crumbs. Arrange the apple slices in an ovenproof dish, adding the brandy marinade. Sprinkle the crumb mixture over the top; cover and bake at 350° for 30 minutes. Uncover and bake 30 minutes more.

Sour Cream Apple Squares

2 cups flour
2 cups brown sugar,
  firmly packed
½ cup butter or margarine,
  softened
1 cup chopped nuts
1-2 teaspoons cinnamon

1 teaspoon baking soda
½ teaspoon salt
½ cup dairy sour cream
1 teaspoon vanilla
1 egg
2 cups peeled & finely
  chopped apples
Whipped cream

Lightly spoon the flour into a measuring cup; level off. In a large bowl combine the first 3 ingredients; blend at low speed until crumbly. Stir in the nuts. Press 2¾ cups crumb mixture into an ungreased 13x9-inch pan. To the remaining mixture, add the cinnamon, soda, salt, sour cream, vanilla, and egg. Blend well. Stir in the apples. Spoon evenly over the base. Bake at 350° for 25-30 minutes until done. Cut into squares. Serve with whipped cream.

Rhubarb Roll-ups

Sauce:
2 cups brown sugar
2 cups water
¼ cup butter
½ teaspoon cinnamon

Roll-ups:
2 cups flour
2½ teaspoons baking powder

½ teaspoon salt
⅔ cup plus 2 tablespoons
   butter
½ cup milk
5 cups finely cut rhubarb
½ cup sugar
½ teaspoon cinnamon
Cream

Sauce: Prepare the sauce by combining the brown sugar, water, butter, and cinnamon. Cook, uncovered, at a rolling boil for 5 minutes. Set aside while preparing the **Roll-ups.**

Roll-ups. Sift the flour, baking powder, and salt. Cut in ⅔ cup butter. Add the milk and mix to a soft dough. Roll out on a floured board to form a rectangle approximately 14x17-inches. Spread with 2 table-spoons butter. Cover with rhubarb. Sprinkle with the sugar mixed with cinnamon. Roll as for a jelly roll. Cut into 1-inch slices. Place cut side down in a greased 13x9x2-inch pan. Pour the prepared **Sauce** over the slices. Bake at 375° for 40 minutes. Serve hot or cold with cream.

Excellent made with scone mix.

Serves 10 to 12.

Ice Cream Soufflé with Strawberries

1 quart vanilla ice cream,
   softened
8 almond macaroons,
   crumbled

6 tablespoons Grand Marnier
¾ cup heavy cream, whipped
1 quart fresh strawberries
½ cup sugar

Let the ice cream stand in the refrigerator 1 hour to soften a little. In a bowl, blend the softened ice cream with the crumbled macaroons, ¼ cup Grand Marnier, and the whipped cream. Freeze in a 9-inch spring-form pan. Allow about 8 hours or overnight for freezing. About an hour before serving time, combine washed, well-drained, hulled, and sliced fresh strawberries with sugar and 2 tablespoons Grand Marnier. Serve the ice cream soufflé with the strawberries.

Serves 6.

Chelan Rum-Baked Apples

4 large Washington Golden Delicious apples
4 tablespoons apricot jam
4 teaspoons chopped almonds
2 tablespoons butter, softened
4 tablespoons sugar

3 tablespoons water
¼ cup rum

Cheese Topping:
1 (3 ounce) package cream cheese, softened
1 tablespoon rum
2 tablespoons apricot jam

Pare and core the apples. Remove the blossom, but leave the bottom intact. Combine the apricot jam, chopped almonds, butter, and sugar. Spoon into the centers of the apples. Combine the water and the rum. Wrap each apple in heavy-duty foil. Before sealing, pour about 2 tablespoons water-rum mixture over each apple. Seal. Bake at 375° for 35-45 minutes or until the apples are tender. Serve warm in foil with **Cheese Topping.**

Cheese Topping: Beat the cream cheese with the rum and apricot jam.

Variation: Grate sharp cheddar cheese over whipped cream as a substitute for **Cheese Topping.**

Serves 4.

Raspberry-Glazed Cheese Torte

2 (10 ounce) packages
  frozen raspberries
1 envelope unflavored
  gelatin
⅓ cup water
⅓ cup sugar
1 teaspoon grated
  lemon peel

1 tablespoon lemon juice
1 pound cottage cheese,
  sieved or pureed
¼ teaspoon salt
1 cup heavy cream, whipped
Slivered toasted almonds
4 teaspoons cornstarch
3 tablespoons sugar
¼ teaspoon almond extract

Thaw and drain the frozen raspberries, reserving the syrup for the glaze. Soften the gelatin in the water. Heat slowly to dissolve. Add the sugar, lemon peel, lemon juice, cottage cheese, and salt. Chill until syrupy. Fold in the whipped cream. Sprinkle the bottom of a buttered 7-inch spring-form pan with almonds, reserving a few for the sides of the torte. Pour in the cheese mixture. Chill until firm. Combine the cornstarch and sugar. Slowly stir in ¾ cup reserved raspberry syrup. Cook over medium heat until thickened and clear, stirring constantly. Stir in the almond extract. Cool to room temperature. Arrange the raspberries over the top of the torte. Cover with the glaze. Chill until firm. Remove the sides of the pan. Cover the sides of the torte with the reserved almonds.

Serves 8.

Girl Scout Lemon Supreme

1 package lemon pudding &
  pie filling (not instant)
½ cup cold water
½ cup sugar
2 eggs, separated
1 (17 ounce) can fruit cocktail,
  drained, reserving the liquid

1 tablespoon unflavored
  gelatin
1 tablespoon lemon juice
½ cup crushed shortbread
  cookies (Girl Scout or
  similar type)
Whipped cream (optional)

Mix the lemon pudding and pie filling with ¼ cup cold water, ¼ cup sugar, and 2 egg yolks, slightly beaten. Add 2 cups liquid (juice from

268

fruit cocktail plus water). Bring to a full rolling boil. Stir in gelatin softened in remaining ¼ cup cold water. Stir to dissolve. Remove from heat and stir in the lemon juice. Let cool for 5 minutes, stirring once or twice. Beat 2 egg whites, gradually adding ¼ cup sugar. Beat until stiff peaks are formed. Gradually fold in the lemon pudding, then gently fold in the well drained fruit cocktail. Use butter or margarine to coat a 8x8x2-inch square cake pan or Pyrex dish. Sprinkle with crushed cookies. Pour the lemon filling into the dish over the crushed cookies. Refrigerate for 3-4 hours or until well set. Serve in squares with or without whipped cream.

Serves 6 to 8.

Baked Chocolate Pudding

1 cup sifted flour
½ teaspoon salt
¾ cup sugar
2 teaspoons baking powder
4½ teaspoons cocoa
2 tablespoons melted butter
1 teaspoon vanilla extract
½ cup milk
½ cup chopped nuts

Cocoa Topping:
½ cup granulated sugar
½ cup brown sugar
6 tablespoons cocoa
1 cup water

Whipped cream

Sift together the first 5 ingredients. Combine the butter, vanilla extract, and milk; then add to the dry mixture. Add the nuts and pour into a buttered 5x9-inch baking dish. Pour the **Cocoa Topping** over the batter in the pan and bake at 350° for 40 minutes. Serve in sherbet glasses with whipped cream.

Cocoa Topping: Combine the sugars and cocoa. Pour the water over the cocoa mixture and stir well.

Serves 6.

Viennese Peach Tart

½ cup butter
¼ cup confectioners sugar
1 cup flour
1 tablespoon cornstarch
2 tablespoons sugar

¼ teaspoon mace or nutmeg
½ cup orange juice
½ cup red currant jelly, melted
8 large fresh peaches
Whipped cream

Prepare the crust by creaming the butter until soft. Add the confectioners sugar gradually, and continue to cream. Blend in the flour to make a soft dough. Pat evenly into a 12-inch torte pan or pizza pan, covering the bottom and sides. Bake at 350° for 20 minutes. Prepare the glaze by combining the cornstarch, sugar, and mace or nutmeg. Add the orange juice. Cook over hot water or low heat, stirring, until thick and clear. Stir in the jelly. Cool slightly. Peel and slice the peaches, and arrange in a single layer in the baked shell. Spoon the glaze evenly over the peaches. Chill. Garnish with whipped cream.

Serves 8 to 10.

Peach Fruit Leather

10 cups pitted &
  sliced peaches

1 cup sugar

Using a food mill or processor, puree the peaches. Pour the peaches into a saucepan and add the sugar. Heat to 180°, and simmer until syrupy, stirring occasionally. Tape sheets of plastic to cardboard or cookie sheets, or grease cookie sheets. Spread a thin layer (approximately ⅛-inch thick) on the prepared cardboard or cookie sheets and dry in the sun or in the oven set at 140-150°. After the fruit has dried down to a slightly tacky state (requires approximately 8 hours), remove and roll up the leather in wax paper or plastic wrap. Store in a container with a tightly fitting lid in a cool location. It will keep 1 month at room temperature, 4 months refrigerated, or 1 year frozen.

Serves 2 hikers for a weekend.

Carrot Pudding

2 pounds carrots, grated
⅓ cup butter
Juice of ½ lemon,
   or to taste
¾ teaspoon salt

1 teaspoon sugar
1½ cups undiluted
   evaporated milk
3 eggs
Dash white pepper

Peel and coarsely grate the carrots or blend them at the grate position in the blender, cutting into chunks and blending a small amount at a time. (You may also use a food mill with a medium blade.) In a sauce-pan, add the carrots, butter, lemon juice, ½ teaspoon salt, sugar, and enough water to barely cover. Bring to a simmer and cook, covered, for about 10 minutes or until tender. Uncover and stir, cooking until the water is evaporated. Cool. In a bowl, whisk together the undiluted evaporated milk, eggs, ¼ teaspoon salt, and white pepper. Stir into the carrots. Pour into a buttered 10x6x1¾-inch baking dish, and bake at 350° for about 30-35 minutes or until the surface is puffed and brown.

Serves 6.

Quick & Easy Brandied Fruits

1 (30 ounce) can fruit cocktail
1 stick cinnamon

4 whole cloves
¾ cup sugar
⅔ cup brandy

Drain the syrup from the fruit cocktail into a sauce pan. Set the fruit aside. Add the cinnamon, cloves, and sugar to the syrup and boil for 5 minutes. Add the fruit and bring to boil again. Pour the brandy, ⅓ cup each, into 2 sterilized pint jars. Spoon in the fruit and pour over enough syrup mixture to bring within ½-inch of the rim. Place two cloves in each jar. Break the cinnamon stick in half, and place one half in each jar. Seal and decorate for the table or as a gift. Flavor improves with a few days aging. Serve over ice cream, angel, pound, or plain cake. Use as a sauce with custard or other desserts.

Makes 4 cups.

Frozen Macaroon Soufflé

1 quart vanilla ice cream
12 almond macaroons,
   crumbled
3 tablespoons Grand Marnier
2 cups heavy cream, whipped

Raspberry Sauce:
2 (10 ounce) packages
   frozen raspberries
5 tablespoons sugar
3 tablespoons Grand Marnier

Soften the ice cream. Stir the crumbled macaroons and the Grand Marnier into the ice cream. Fold in half of the whipped cream. Spoon into a 6 cup metal mold. Cover with plastic wrap and freeze. When ready to serve, unmold by running a knife around the edge, then dipping the mold quickly in hot water. Pour **Raspberry Sauce** over the soufflé and garnish with the remaining whipped cream.

Raspberry Sauce: Simmer the frozen raspberries until soft; then add the sugar. Cool. Stir in the Grand Marnier.

Serves 12.

Plum Kuchen

½ cup butter
1¾ cups sugar
1¼ cups sifted flour
½ teaspoon salt
½ teaspoon cinnamon

¼ teaspoon baking powder
3 cups diced, fresh plums
1 cup sour cream
1 egg, well beaten

In a mixing bowl, cream the butter. Gradually add 1 cup sugar, beating until light and fluffy. Sift together the flour, salt, cinnamon, and baking powder. Gradually add to the creamed mixture (it will be crumbly). Set aside ⅓ cup. Press the remainder to cover the bottom and extend 1-inch up the sides of an 8-inch square pan. Arrange the plums in this shell. Sprinkle with ¾ cup sugar and ⅓ cup butter/flour mixture. Bake at 400° for 15 minutes. Whip the sour cream until doubled in volume, then fold in the egg. Pour over the plums. Bake 30 minutes more. Serve warm.

Serves 6 to 8.

Peach Kuchen

2 cups sifted flour
¼ teaspoon baking powder
½ teaspoon salt
1 cup sugar
1 cup butter or margarine

2-3 fresh peaches, sliced
 (2 cups)
1 teaspoon cinnamon
2 egg yolks
1 cup heavy or sour cream

Sift the flour, baking powder, salt, and 2 tablespoons of sugar together. Cut in the butter or margarine until the mixture resembles corn meal. Pat the mixture over the bottom and up the sides of an 8-inch square pan to form a shell. Arrange the peaches in the shell, overlapping. Combine the cinnamon and remaining sugar; sprinkle over the peaches. Bake 15 minutes at 400°. Mix the egg yolks and cream slightly; pour the mixture over the top. Bake 30 minutes longer.

Serves 8.

Grapenut Pudding

1 cup Grapenuts
1 cup boiling water
1 cup sugar
1 cup raisins
2 cups diced apples
½ cup chopped pecans

1 teaspoon cinnamon
1 teaspoon nutmeg
1 teaspoon ground cloves
1 tablespoon melted butter
Whipped cream or ice cream

Combine the Grapenuts, boiling water, sugar, raisins, diced apples, pecans, cinnamon, nutmeg, cloves, and melted butter. Spoon into a baking dish. Bake at 350° for 1 hour. Serve warm with whipped cream or ice cream.

Serves 4.

Pies

Peanut Butter Pie

3 ounces cream cheese,
  softened
1 cup powdered sugar
⅓ cup milk

½ cup peanut butter
½ teaspoon vanilla
9 ounces Cool Whip
Graham cracker or vanilla
  wafer crumb crust

Beat the cream cheese until light and fluffy. Beat in the sugar, milk, peanut butter, and vanilla. Fold in the Cool Whip, and pour into the pie crust. Keep in the freezer and serve it right from the freezer.

Serves 6 to 8.

Pink Wine Chiffon Pie

4 eggs, separated
⅓ cup Flame' Pink Table Wine
⅔ cup sugar
1 envelope unflavored gelatin
¼ teaspoon salt

1 cup whipping cream
¼ teaspoon vanilla
Red food coloring
1 (9-inch) graham cracker
  crust

Mix the egg yolks in a heavy saucepan with the Flame' Pink Table Wine and ⅓ cup sugar. Sprinkle the unflavored gelatin over the egg yolk mixture. Allow to soften. Cook over low heat, stirring constantly, until the gelatin is thickened (will coat a spoon), about 5 minutes. Remove from the heat; cool slightly. Gelatin should not set. Beat the egg whites and the salt at high speed until soft peaks form. Gradually sprinkle in ⅓ cup sugar, beating at high speed until the sugar is completely dissolved. Beat the whipping cream and the vanilla at medium speed until stiff peaks form. Gently fold the egg yolk mixture into the egg whites; then fold in the whipped cream. Add red food coloring until a desired color is obtained. Fold until evenly mixed. Spoon the mixture into a baked 9-inch graham cracker crust. Refrigerate until set, at least 5 hours.

Serves 8.

Pumpkin Ice Cream Pie

1 (9-inch) pastry shell
1 pint vanilla ice cream
1 cup canned pumpkin
¾ cup sugar
½ teaspoon salt

½ teaspoon ginger
½ teaspoon cinnamon
¼ teaspoon nutmeg
1 cup whipping cream,
  whipped

Prepare and bake the pastry shell. Spoon the vanilla ice cream over the bottom of the pastry shell. Freeze. Combine the pumpkin, sugar, salt, and spices. Fold in the whipped cream. Spread the pumpkin mixture over the ice cream-filled pastry shell. Freeze. Allow 20-30 minutes in the refrigerator before serving.

Serves 6 to 8.

Fresh Peach Upside-Down Pie

2 tablespoons butter
⅔ cup toasted almonds
  or pecans
⅓ cup brown sugar
Pastry for a 2-crust pie
5 cups peeled, sliced
  fresh peaches

¾ cup sugar
¼ cup brown sugar
2 tablespoons tapioca
½ teaspoon nutmeg
¼ teaspoon cinnamon
Milk
Whipped cream or ice cream

Line a 9-inch pie pan with a 12-inch square of foil. Let the excess foil overhang the edge. Spread the inside of the foil-lined pan with the butter. Press the nuts and brown sugar into the butter. Prepare pastry for a two-crust pie. Fit the bottom crust into the pan over the nuts. Mix peeled and sliced fresh peaches with sugar, brown sugar, tapioca, nutmeg, and cinnamon. Pour into the crust and cover with the top crust. Seal and prick with a fork. Brush lightly with milk. Bake at 450° for 10 minutes; then lower the temperature to 375°, and bake 35-40 minutes or until done. Cool. Turn upside down on a serving plate. Remove the foil. Serve with whipped cream or ice cream.

Serves 6 to 8.

Black Bottom Pie

Crust:
1½ cups fine graham cracker
   or Zwieback crumbs
¼ cups confectioners sugar
6 tablespoons butter, melted
1 teaspoon cinnamon

Filling:
1 tablespoon gelatin
¼ cup cold water
2 cups milk
¾ cup sugar

4 teaspoons cornstarch
4 egg yolks, lightly beaten
1½ ounces (1½ squares)
   unsweetened chocolate,
   melted
½ teaspoon vanilla
3 tablespoons rum
3 egg whites
¼ teaspoon salt
¼ teaspoon cream of tartar
1 cup heavy cream
2 tablespoons confectioners
   sugar

Crust: Combine the graham cracker or Zwieback crumbs with the confectioners sugar, melted butter, and cinnamon. Reserve ½ cup of this mixture for the topping. Place the remainder in a 9-inch pan and press firmly against the bottom and sides of the pan. Bake at 375° for 15 minutes.

Filling: Soak the gelatin in the cold water. Set aside. Heat the milk to the scalding point. Stir in ½ cup sugar mixed with cornstarch, then the egg yolks. Stir and cook over low heat or over water for about 20 minutes or until the custard will coat a spoon heavily. Take out 1 cup of the custard and add the melted chocolate to it. Beat until well blended and cool. Add the vanilla. Pour this into the pie shell. Dissolve the soaked gelatin in the remaining custard (be sure it's hot!). Let it cool, but don't permit it to set. When cool, stir in the rum. Beat the egg whites with salt until well blended. Add the cream of tartar. Beat until the egg whites are stiff. Beat in gradually ¼ cup sugar. Fold into the custard. Spoon the custard into the pie shell. Whip the heavy cream until stiff, gradually adding 2 tablespoons confectioners sugar. Cover the custard with the whipped cream. Sprinkle the remaining ½ cup crumbs over the top.

Serves 6 to 8.

Yakima Cheese Crumble Apple Pie

Crumble Topping:
2 (5½ ounce) sticks
 pie crust mix, divided
½ cup sugar
½ cup brown sugar,
 firmly packed
¾ teaspoon cinnamon
3 tablespoons butter

2 cups shredded cheddar
 cheese
Remainder of pie cust mix
2-2½ tablespoons water
3 pounds cooking apples,
 peeled & sliced
1 tablespoon flour
Freshly grated nutmeg

Crumble Topping: Measure 1 cup of pie crust mix and combine with sugars and cinnamon. Cut in butter thoroughly. Set aside.

Mix 1 cup cheddar cheese into the remaining pie crust mix. Blend with the water. Roll the dough, and line a 9-inch pie plate. Place the apples in the pastry-lined pie plate, sprinkling flour evenly over them. Sprinkle with nutmeg, and cover with half of the **Crumble Topping.** Sprinkle the remaining 1 cup cheddar cheese over all. Top with the remaining **Crumble Topping.** Bake at 400° for 10 minutes, then at 350° for 40-50 minutes, until the topping is golden brown and apples are tender.

Strawberry Cheese Pie

1(8 ounce) package
 cream cheese
3 tablespoons cream
1 baked (9-inch) pie shell,
 cooled

1 quart strawberries
2 heaping tablespoons
 cornstarch
Pineapple juice
¾ cup sugar
Whipped cream

Blend the cream cheese and cream together, then spread on the cooled pie shell. Chill. Wash and hull the berries. Slice half of the largest berries. Mash the other half and put through a sieve to make a puree. Add cornstarch to this and mix to a paste. Add enough pineapple juice to make 1½ cups liquid. Add the sugar, and cook until thick and transparent, stirring constantly. Cool. Pour ½ into a pie shell, and arrange sliced berries on it. Pour on the rest and chill. Serve with whipped cream.

Peaches n' Cream Pie

½ cup butter
1 ½ cups flour
¼ cup water, approximately
1 tablespoon grated or finely
  minced almonds
1 tablespoon fine, dry
  bread crumbs

4 medium fresh peaches
2 cups light cream
3 egg yolks
3 whole eggs
½ teaspoon nutmeg
⅛ teaspoon salt
½ cup sugar
2 tablespoons butter, melted

Cut the butter into the flour with a pastry blender. Add just enough water to hold the mixture together. Shape into a ball, roll out, and fit in a 10-inch piepan. Fold the edges under and flute. Sprinkle almonds and bread crumbs into the shell. Peel and thinly slice the fresh peaches over the bread crumbs. Bake at 375° for 10 minutes. Beat the light cream, egg yolks, whole eggs, nutmeg, and salt together, then pour over the peaches. Bake at 350° for 30 minutes or until firm. Sprinkle with sugar and pour the melted butter over the top. Put in a 450° oven for about 5 minutes, until the sugar melts and lightly browns. Serve hot or cold.

Serves 6 to 8.

Brandied Pumpkin Pie

1 cup canned pumpkin
1 cup evaporated milk
1 cup light brown sugar,
  firmly packed
3 eggs, slightly beaten
¼ cup brandy

1 teaspoon pumpkin pie spice
  (or 1 teaspoon cinnamon,
  ½ teaspoon ginger,
  ¼ teaspoon cloves)
¾ teaspoon salt
1 (9-inch) almond pastry shell

Prepare the filling by combining the pumpkin, milk, and sugar in a large bowl and blending until well mixed. Stir in the eggs, brandy, pie spice, and salt; mix well. Pour the filling into the prepared pie shell. Bake at 400° for 50-55 minutes, or until the tip of a knife inserted in the center comes out clean. Cool on a wire rack. Serve with whipped cream.

Cherry Cheese Pie

1 (3 ounce) package black
   cherry flavored gelatin
1 cup hot water
1 cup cold water or
   fruit juice
2 cups dark sweet cherries

1 (3 ounce) package cream
   cheese
1 or 2 tablespoons cream
Baked pie shell
Whipped cream

Dissolve the gelatin in the hot water. Add the cold water or fruit juice. Chill until syrupy. Wash, pit, and halve the cherries. Blend the cream cheese with the cream and spread over the baked pie shell. Combine the cherries and gelatin. Pour into the cheese-lined shell. Chill until set. Garnish with whipped cream.

Serves 6 to 8.

Strawberry Chiffon Pie

1 tablespoon gelatin
¼ cup water
4 eggs, separated
¾ cup sugar
1 tablespoon lemon juice
½ teaspoon salt

1 cup strawberry pulp &
   juice
Red food coloring
1 (9-inch) baked pie shell
Whipped cream

Soak the gelatin in ¼ cup cold water for 5 minutes. Beat the egg yolks slightly, and add ½ cup sugar, lemon juice, and salt. Cook over boiling water or on very low heat, stirring constantly, until of custard consistency. Add the softened gelatin, stirring thoroughly to dissolve. Add the strawberry pulp and juice and a little red coloring to give a pleasing color. Cool, and when the mixture begins to congeal, fold in the stiffly beaten egg whites to which ¼ cup sugar has been added. Fill the pie shell and chill. Before serving, spread a thin layer of whipped cream over the pie and garnish with strawberries.

Serves 6 to 8.

Sour Cream Raisin Pie

1 cup brown sugar,
  firmly packed
2 tablespoons flour
½ teaspoon nutmeg
½ teaspoon cinnamon
¼ teaspoon salt
1 cup sour cream
3 egg yolks
1 cup raisins

1 (9-inch) pie shell, baked

Meringue:
3 egg whites
⅛ teaspoon salt
6 tablespoons sugar

Combine the brown sugar, flour, nutmeg, cinnamon, salt, and sour cream in the top of a double boiler on very low heat and cook until thick, stirring all the time. Beat the egg yolks and blend a little of the hot sauce with them before stirring into the mixture. Cook for 2-3 minutes more, then add the raisins. Cool. Place in baked 9-inch pie shell and cover to the edges with **Meringue.**

Meringue: Beat the egg whites with salt to a stiff foam. Add the sugar gradually in portions of 1 tablespoon at a time, beating well after each addition. Continue beating until the meringue is very thick and glossy and the sugar is completely dissolved. Spread on the pie, being careful to seal the crust all around. Bake at 350° for 12-15 minutes or until a delicate golden brown.

Serves 6 to 8.

Fluffy Lime Pie

1 envelope unflavored gelatin
¼ cup cold water
3 eggs, separated
1 cup sugar

½ cup lime juice
1 teaspoon grated lime rind
Baked pie shell
Whipped cream, sweetened

Soften the gelatin in the water. Cook the egg yolks and ½ cup sugar over boiling water, stirring constantly, until thickened. Add the gelatin, and stir until dissolved. Add the lime juice and lime rind. Cool. Beat the egg whites and ½ cup sugar to form peaks. Fold into the custard. Pour into a baked pie shell. Chill and serve with sweetened whipped cream.

Serves 6 to 8.

Apricot Fluff Pie

1 tablespoon gelatin
¾ cup cold water
2 cups coarsely cut apricots
2 eggs, separated
1 cup plus 2 tablespoons
    sugar

½ teaspoon salt
1 tablespoon lemon juice
1 (9 inch) pie shell, baked
Whipped cream

Soften the gelatin in ¼ cup cold water. Wash, pit, and coarsely cut enough apricots to make 2 cups. Add ½ cup water. Bring to a boil and simmer for 1 minute. Mash with a fork or blend to a smooth pulp. Combine 2 egg yolks, 1 cup sugar, salt, apricot pulp, and lemon juice. Cook over low heat until thick, stirring constantly. Add the gelatin; stir until dissolved. Cool until slightly set. Beat 2 egg whites and gradually add 2 tablespoons sugar. Combine with the apricot mixture. Fill the pastry shell. Chill. Top with whipped cream.

Serves 6 to 8.

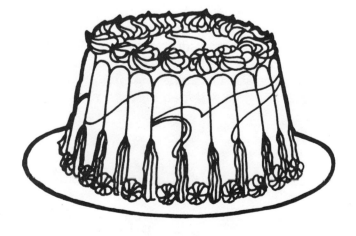

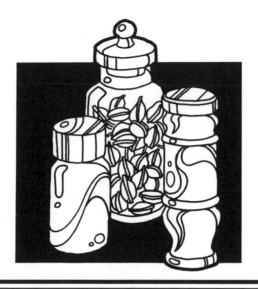

Old Favorites

After Ski Deep Dish Pizza

1 pound ground beef
¼ cup chopped onion
¼ cup chopped green pepper
1 (16 ounce) can tomatoes

1 package cheese pizza
2 (6 ounce) packages natural,
   low-moisture, part-skim
   mozzarella cheese slices
Parmesan cheese

Brown the meat; drain. Add the onion and green pepper; cook until tender. Stir in the tomatoes, pizza sauce, and herb spice mix; simmer 15 minutes. Prepare the pizza dough as directed on the package. With fingers greased, press onto the bottom and halfway up the sides of a greased 13x9-inch pan. Cover with half of the mozzarella cheese and half of the meat sauce; repeat with the remaining cheese and meat sauce. Sprinkle with the grated Parmesan cheese. Bake at 425° for 20-25 minutes. Let stand 10 minutes before serving.

What could be more appetizing to those who come in out of the cold than this steaming hot pizza?

Seasoned Croutons

1 (1 pound) loaf sour dough
   French bread
1 cup butter,
2 medium cloves garlic
¼ teaspoon sage
¼ teaspoon pepper

¼ teaspoon ground
   celery seed
½ teaspoon finely
   crushed oregano
½ teaspoon seasoned salt
1 cup chopped parsley
5 ounces dry sherry (optional)

Cut the bread into ½-inch cubes. Put the cubes on a cookie sheet and bake at 375° until light brown and crisp, about 12-15 minutes. Put the bread aside in large mixing bowl. In a saucepan, melt the butter and sauté the garlic. When the garlic is brown, discard. Add all the seasonings to the remaining butter. Pour this over the toasted bread cubes, and stir until the butter and seasonings are evenly distributed. If desired, sprinkle with dry sherry. Reduce heat to 350° and bake 20-25 minutes or until crisp. Serve as an appetizer or use in soups and salads.

Makes 7 cups croutons.

Cornish Pasties

1 package pie crust mix
¾ pound top round steak,
   pounded thin & minced, or
   lean ground beef
1 cup finely diced raw potato
½ medium onion,
   finely chopped

1 teaspoon salt
¼ teaspoon pepper
⅛ teaspoon nutmeg
2 tablespoons finely
   chopped parsley
1 egg, beaten with
   1 tablespoon water

Prepare the pie crust according to package directions. Chill. Combine the meat, potato, onion, seasonings, and parsley. Roll out the pie crust and cut into 6 rounds, each about 6-inches in diameter (use a saucer or small plate as a cutting guide). Put a generous portion of the meat mixture on half of each round. Brush the edge of the round with the beaten egg, fold the pastry over, and press the edges together to seal. Cut a small opening in the top crust and brush the surface with beaten egg. Bake at 400° for 15 minutes. Reduce heat to 350° and bake 30 minutes more.

Makes 6 pasties.

Luncheon Sandwich

⅔ cup deviled ham
2 teaspoons instant onion
¼ pound grated
   processed cheese
4 tablespoons hamburger
   relish

4 tablespoons finely chopped
   green pepper
2 tablespoons catsup
6 frankfurter buns, sliced
6 (1 ounce) slices
   processed cheese

Combine the deviled ham, onion, grated cheese, relish, green pepper, and catsup. Spread 3 tablespoons of the mixture on each half of the frankfurter buns. Cut the 6 slices of cheese into 4 strips each. Place the strips on each half of the buns. Heat the bun halves on a baking sheet at 350° for 10 minutes. Serve with fruit or vegetable salad.

Serves 6.

North-of-the-Border Enchiladas

4 soft corn tortillas
½ cup old-fashioned
   peanut butter
1 ripe avocado, peeled,
   pitted, & mashed

1 cup shredded lettuce
1 ripe tomato, chopped
¼ cup sliced green onion
1 cup grated cheddar cheese
Hot taco sauce

Spread the tortillas with the peanut butter, then the avocado. Sprinkle with the lettuce, tomato, and onion. Roll up. Place seam-side down in a baking dish. Sprinkle with the cheese. Bake, uncovered, at 375° for 10-15 minutes until the cheese melts. Serve with hot sauce.

Serves 4.

Old-Fashioned Bread Dressing

½ cup butter or margarine
1 cup finely chopped onion
1 cup finely chopped celery
¼ cup finely chopped
   celery leaves
2 tablespoons finely chopped
   parsley
3 quarts dried bread cubes

½-1 cup giblet broth, cold
½ teaspoon salt
1 teaspoon poultry seasoning
½ teaspoon ground or
   crushed rosemary
½ teaspoon thyme
½ teaspoon pepper

Melt the butter or margarine. Cook the onion, celery, celery leaves, and parsley until tender. Mix with the bread cubes. Add the giblet broth a little at a time. Moisten the outside of the cubes but leave the inside crisp. Add the salt, poultry seasoning, rosemary, thyme, and pepper. Mix well. Taste and correct the seasonings. Lightly stuff the bird just before putting it in the oven.

Extra stuffing can be baked in a buttered casserole. Add a little extra broth. Bake, covered, at 325° to 350° for 30 minutes. Uncover and cook an additional 15 minutes.

Makes 12 cups.

Quick Pizza

2 cups sifted flour
⅓ cup instant nonfat dry milk
2½ teaspoons baking powder
½ teaspoon salt
6 tablespoons butter
⅔ cup water

1 (6 ounce) can tomato paste
½ teaspoon garlic salt
½ teaspoon ground oregano
Dash pepper
3 cups shredded cheddar
  cheese

Sift together the flour, dry milk, baking powder, and salt. Cut in the butter until the dough is the texture of coarse corn meal. Add the water and stir with a fork until the dough follows the fork around in the bowl. Turn out on a lightly floured board and knead gently about 30 seconds. Divide the dough in half. Roll each half into a 10-inch circle or into a 10x12-inch rectangle. Place on a buttered baking sheet and turn up the edges slightly. Mix the tomato paste with the garlic salt, oregano, and pepper. Spread half on each piece of dough. Add one of the **Variations** listed below. Sprinkle the cheddar cheese on top. Bake at 425° for about 15 minutes.

Variations:
1 can tuna, drained & flaked
½ pound bologna, chopped
8 slices pepperoni, chopped
8 slices bacon, fried crisp
    & crumbled
6-8 stuffed olives, sliced
½ pound ground beef

1 can crab, drained & flaked
8 slices salami, chopped
1 (2 ounce) can mushroom
    pieces, drained
4 pork sausages, fried &
    thinly sliced
4-5 hot dogs, thinly sliced

Serves 4 to 6.

Home-Made Mustard

1 cup white vinegar
4 ounces dry mustard
1 cup sugar

2 eggs, well beaten
1 teaspoon salt
1½ cups mayonnaise

Gradually stir the vinegar into the mustard in a saucepan. Add the sugar, eggs, and salt. Cook over medium heat until thick. Cool, then add mayonnaise. Refrigerate.

This mustard keeps well in the refrigerator and is delicious with ham, on sandwiches, and with any other foods requiring a touch of mustard.

Makes 2 to 3 cups.

Shake & Bake

2 cups dry bread crumbs
¼ cup flour
1 tablespoon paprika
  (more, if desired)
4 teaspoons salt

2 teaspoons sugar
2 teaspoons onion powder
2 teaspoons ground oregano
½ teaspoon garlic powder
¼ cup shortening

Mix the dry ingredients thoroughly. Cut in the shortening until the mixture is crumbly. Store in a tightly covered container. Use about ⅓ cup per pound of fish, 1 cup for chicken and chops. Dip fish, chicken or chops into milk, then into the coating. Place in a single layer in an ungreased, shallow baking dish. Bake fish at 400° for 5-10 minutes or until tender and brown. Bake chicken at 350° for 45-50 minutes. Bake chops at 325° for 1 hour, or until done.

Makes 2⅔ cups.

Granola

2 cups oatmeal
1 cup 4-Grain Cereal Mates
½ cup wheat germ
¼ cup sesame seeds
1 cup coconut

1 cup chopped or sliced
  almonds
½ cup brown sugar
2 teaspoons vanilla
1 cup chopped dried apples
1 cup light raisins

Mix together the oatmeal, cereal mates (equal amounts of wheat, rye, oats, and barley), wheat germ, sesame seeds, coconut, almonds, brown sugar, and vanilla. Place in a large pan and bake at 275° for 30 minutes. Then stir well and add the apples. Place back in the oven and let the cereal toast for 30 minutes more, stirring every 10 minutes. Remove from the oven and add the raisins. Stir well and cool. Store in a tightly covered container in the refrigerator. To serve, top with milk or cream.

Makes 7 cups.

Peanut Butter Banana Granola

3 ripe medium bananas
3 cups oatmeal
1 cup wheat germ
1 cup bran
1 cup shredded coconut
1 cup peanuts

½ cup packed brown sugar
2 teaspoons ground cinnamon
¼ teaspoon salt
¾ cup chunky peanut butter
¼ cup vegetable oil*
2 teaspoons vanilla

Peel and slice the bananas into a blender. Whir until pureed (should have at least 1½ cups). Mix the dry ingredients in a large bowl. Stir together the banana, peanut butter, oil, and vanilla. Pour over the dry mixture and stir until thoroughly moist. Spread in a 9x15-inch baking pan. Bake at 325° for about 1 hour and 15 minutes, stirring occasionally until granola is dry and crisp.

*Use the oil from the old-fashioned peanut butter plus what is needed in vegetable oil.

Makes about 2 quarts.

Teen's Snack Pack

2 cups uncooked rolled oats
1 cup wheat germ
¾ cup raisins
½ cup shredded coconut
½ cup chopped & pitted dates
½ cup sunflower seeds
½ cup slivered almonds
2 tablespoons sesame seeds

1 cup diced, dried apples
½ cup teaspoon salt
½ cup light brown sugar, packed
⅓ cup vegetable oil
½ cup frozen, concentrated orange juice
1 teaspoon vanilla

In a large bowl, combine the rolled oats, wheat germ, raisins, coconut, dates, sunflower seeds, almonds, sesame seeds, apples, and salt. Mix thoroughly, separating the dates. In another bowl, mix the brown sugar, vegetable oil, orange juice (thawed and undiluted), and vanilla. Add to the cereal mixture and mix. Separate the dates well. Spread the mixture on two jelly roll pans. Bake at 300° for 40-45 minutes or until golden brown and crisp. Stir every 10 minutes. Cool. Divide into ½ cup portions and seal in small plastic bags or store in a covered container.

Makes 16 (½ cup) portions.

Brandied Fruit

6 cups ripe, firm strawberries, washed, drained, & capped
6 cups sugar
1 pint brandy
1 pint kirsch
1 pint sweet sherry wine
2 sticks cinnamon

1 tablespoon whole cloves
1 tablespoon whole allspice
1 tablespoon grated lemon rind
1 tablespoon grated orange rind
1 tablespoon grated green ginger root

Crush the berries to a fine pulp or put through a blender. Add the sugar and stir until it is dissolved. Heat to simmering point; do not boil. Cool the syrup. Add the liquors, spices (which have been tied in a cheese cloth bag), and other ingredients. Put into a sterilized 4-6 gallon crock with close-fitting cover. Let this mixture stand for at least one week.

As fresh fruits are available, add equal quantities of fresh fruit and sugar, stirring after each addition. Do not cook. Never add more than 2 quarts of fruit at one time or in one week. For each 2 quarts of fruit and 2 quarts of sugar, add 1 pint of brandy. For smaller proportions, use 1 cup fruit, 1 cup sugar, and ¼ cup brandy. Another bag of spices may be added after a couple of months if needed.

If a richer red syrup is desired, use red cherries, red raspberries, red plums, peaches, and so on. Continue to add fruit, sugar, and brandy until the crock is filled or until you have the amount of brandied fruit you want. Keep the cover on the crock or cover with foil AT ALL TIMES. By the end of the summer, you will enjoy the fruit. The fruit and juice may be sealed in sterilized jars or allowed to remain in the crock until the holiday season.

Brandied Fruit is delicious served by itself, but it may also be served flaming, over ice cream, cheesecake, or crêpes, as a topping for ham, cake, or in anyway in which a sauce might be used.

Frozen berries, thawed, may be used, but remember they have approximately ¼ cup sugar per (10-ounce) package. Subtract this amount from the sugar you use.

"Happiness is 2 or 3 spoonfuls over ice cream."   **Katherine Wise**

INDEX

Appetizers

Beverages

Seafood

Salmon

INDEX

Poultry

INDEX

INDEX

INDEX

INDEX

Fruit & Puddings

Pies

Old Favorites

NOTES

NOTES

ABOUT THE AUTHOR

You may have heard KOMO announcers refer to Katherine Wise as "The Happy Cooker," and that she is!

Katherine Wise is really home economist Ruth Fratt. Her love for cooking began as a child in Cedar Rapids, Nebraska. She received her B.S. in Home Economics from the University of Nebraska. She traveled to Seattle shortly thereafter to conduct a cooking school, married, and raised two sons. While she cooked for her family she was also busy doing much more: She was "Dorothy Neighbors," home economist writer, for eight years at the Seattle Times. In 1947 she joined KOMO Radio and Television to become the first full time home economist on Seattle radio, offering her recipe service to hundreds of listeners throughout the day. Those hundreds have turned into hundreds of thousands. There have been some months when the station has received up to twenty thousand calls for Katherine's recipes!

Ruth Fratt has made innumerable achievements and contributions through the years. Significantly, Ruth pioneered areas of consumer protection before such organizations were heard of, advocating childbirth education before the word "pregnant" was allowed on the air! She served on numerous boards and commissions and has enriched the lives of those who have worked for her, listened to her and watched her on television. Always placing those in need as a top priority, Ruth has made it a point to take food to rehabilitation houses including much of what she prepared on her TV show, and she has been active and unselfish in providing transportation to the disabled for their daily chores.

Ruth helped make correct labeling (grade and type) of meat mandatory in the marketplace. She worked toward tightening meat inspection rules to prevent ungraded meat from getting to public market. And along with the Food and Drug Administration, she was instrumental in preventing distribution of a dishwasher detergent packaged in a milk carton, fearful the packaging could be potentially harmful in leading children to believe it might be a new drink.

In this book Ruth Fratt offers the best of Katherine Wise recipes, those her listeners have phoned for most often, and special favorites of her own. So cook and enjoy—nothing could make the "Happy Cooker" happier!

···

Cooking with Katherine Wise

To order additional copies of **Cooking with Katherine Wise** please return this form with $9.95 plus $2.00 taxes, postage and handling for each book to **Peanut Butter Publishing**, 2445 76th Avenue S.E., Mercer Island, WA 98040.

Name _____

Address _____ State _____ Zip _____

Visa # _____ Expiration Date _____

MasterCard #_____ Expiration Date _____

Signature _____

Payment enclosed: $_____for _____ copies.

···

Cooking with Katherine Wise

To order additional copies of **Cooking with Katherine Wise** please return this form with $9.95 plus $2.00 taxes, postage and handling for each book to **Peanut Butter Publishing**, 2445 76th Avenue S.E., Mercer Island, WA 98040.

Name _____

Address _____ State _____ Zip _____

Visa # _____ Expiration Date _____

MasterCard #_____ Expiration Date _____

Signature _____

Payment enclosed: $_____for _____ copies.

···